1

Pete's Progress

or

Someone We Love Had Cancer

by

Elizabeth F. Boardman

First published in 2009.

Second edition 2013.

ISBN-13-978-1490308609

Biography. Cancer. Hospice. Family.

Printed in the USA

Dedicated

to Chris,

proud and passionate

son and father.

Acknowledgements

This is a family story told by family and friends, and it would not have been created without them.

Others read through the manuscript with red pencil in hand and made useful editorial suggestions of many sorts. Many thanks for this service to my sisters and to Mary deLap, Fran Peavey, and Gloria Valoris.

Pete's Progress

Table of Contents

Pete's Progress

Introduction and Who's Who

Pete was a city bus driver in up-state New Hampshire when he was first diagnosed with colon cancer in October 2004. This was a man, only sixty years old, who had already survived many career reversals, lived for decades in near poverty, lost a wife, a daughter, and a grandchild, and struggled with many family challenges. His five siblings sometimes called him Job. But he was content and unafraid when he died, his to-do list completed, his soul at peace. His family gathered around, came to understand that Pete was OK, made progress along with him.

Pete was the fourth of six children raised by a small-town family doctor and wife. Among the six of them, he was always the maverick, the independent thinker, the school drop-out. He lived poor almost on purpose. He adopted many of his nine children, and half of those across racial lines. He was their sole parent much of their childhood. He persued his Christian faith intensely for a decade, and then lost it all. But he took everything in stride. If he no longer felt "forgiven" for questionable decisions, he knew with certainty that "it didn't matter."

How did Pete learn to write so well? Almost immediately after he got the cancer diagnosis, he started sending good-humored, educational "updates" by e-email to friends and family describing his doctor visits and his state of mind. They heard about his surgery, the grueling weeks after chemotherapy, the alternative therapies he tried. He wrote a tribute to the small town where he lived that was published in their local paper. His "tool box" paper described for his children tools for life that he had found useful. During periods of respite from chemo, he wrote about mowing the lawn, replacing a roof, touring the county on his motorcycle, and attending a son's death and a daughter's wedding. He wrote a statement of belief and hope to his great granddaughter, baby Lucelia.

Ever the mystery man, the one thing he did not write about was how he had sued his primary physician doctor for early misdiagnosis of the cancer. He just mentioned it once or twice in phone conversations.

As the months passed, Pete's six children, five siblings and other relatives and friends followed his example by keeping in touch by e-mail. In their exchanges, several sub-plots were played out.

- Will Pete be able to die peacefully? At home?
- Who will be with him in the last weeks?
- What will happen if he wins the suit against the doctor?
- What are the family communication problems?
- Will Pete accept hospice care?
- Will people be overwhelmed by grief?
- How will the family handle the funeral?
- What family secrets and issues will be revealed?
- Will the family home have to be sold?
- What will help everyone recover from this loss?

Many honest and lively e-mail messages on these subjects were sent and saved. With names and places changed, many of them are shared here.

Since families everywhere have similar challenges when a parent dies, it seemed that others might benefit from the experience of this familiy. They learned something new every day and hope readers will learn something new on every page about the complex ways that a death in the family affects everyone concerned..

The e-mail correspondance got more frequent and intense as the day of Pete's death approached. After the funeral, it slowly faded away as the family accepted that there was not much more they could do. They returned to their own preoccupations, remembering Pete's own adage: "Take the best, forget the rest."

Who's Who

Pete's siblings are Elinor, Hunter, Sarah (his twin), Caro and Holly. They live all over the country.

Pete had nine children altogether, some by birth, some by adoption, most Caucasian like him, Sonny and Gordie of African American descent.   His children at the time of his death were Terrie, Janeane, Willa, Gordon, Sonny, Jill, and Karen Kay.

He was proud of having many grandchildren and even a great granddaughter, Lucelia.

Pete shared his daily life with five different women over the decades. One got side-tracked by emotional disabilities, and one died unexpectedly young of an inherited illness. Pete was single at the time of his death.

Many other family members and friends appear briefly in this story and are identified if necessary as they go by.

Pete's Progress

Chapter 1: The Good Fight

At first, in summer 2004, Pete's family doctor thought he just had hemorrhoids. But Pete kept going back with questions and eventually insisted on a second opinion. The oncologist performed surgery within a month. As he learned about the disease and the treatments, Pete started sending his good-humored periodic updates about how things were progressing. People were interested, and more and more got on his e-list.

Update 19, Friday, May 6, 2005.

Here I am, eating my Maypo and thinking about doing another update to depress you all.

Actually, there has been some good news, I don't have to take Coumiden tablets or Lovenex injections for the rest of the weekend. The CT scan on Tuesday showed no lymph node involvement. On Thursday, the doctor reported that my CEA [carncinoembyonic antigen] was down to 7 (from 67 in December).

What the CT scan did show was two blood clots. Tuesday afternoon I got a call saying come in to the oncology clinic with your care giver and the medicine which you pick up at the pharmacy. One clot was still in my upper leg, the other in my abdomen. I guess they were worried that one might get to

19

my lungs, heart or brain. So Terrie and I went in and she learned how to administer belly sticks twice a day.

Well, today I went in to the oncology clinic for "labs" and this afternoon I got the good news. … My body had absorbed the blood thinners very efficiently…On Monday morning, I go in for more labs to see how I am doing. The nurse admonished me not to cut myself slicing pepperoni. Not a chance. I have hardly been able to eat anything this week. Maybe that is why my body absorbed the medicine so well.

Anyway, the pains have all gone out of my leg and my sleep has been deeper and longer than usual. A truly surprising, and … to the doctor, unfamiliar side effect of the medicines.

I actually mowed the lawns yesterday. Up and at it. I could have had Jim do it, but first I would have had to go out and show him how to move the car over by the barn and hook- up jumper cables to get the mower started. And then I would have had to show him which gas can to use to fill the tank. Then I would have had to show him how to set the controls so the mower wouldn't quit. In a way, it was easier to do it, and it turned out that I felt well enough to finish the job. It is nice to feel better even if I don't feel well. I also did a couple of loads of laundry. I even ate a piece of pizza, but just one. Then I took a nap.

…Terrie and [her partner] Jim still work Friday and Saturday nights. They helped turn my mattress yesterday. Karen is away this weekend. Alexis and Chip came over for a little while yesterday. The grandfather clock stopped last week, so I took the hands and face off to inspect it and it ran until the weights got to the end of their cables. Karen's Aunt Karen called to catch up….

Today is the first day of spring in Medford. The leaves are coming out on the trees. The woods by Caliston Lake were in full foliage two weeks ago.

Eight weeks to go. Five more chemo sessions.

Luv tu yu all. Catch some rays!

Pete

[When you see three little dots, it means some words have been deleted. Square brackets like the ones around this sentence denote an author's comment.]

==

Pete sent this next essay to his e-list on August 20, 2005. His daughter, Janeane, encouraged him to send it to the local paper and they published it a week or so later.

Upstate - Down Home

Medford, New Hampshire

If you want to know where you live, go to the local parade, down on Main Street. (The village chimes tolled three quarters on the fifth hour as I walked along South Street toward Main.) There you will see all the people. Old people love it that they can sit in their front yards and see the world go by. Young parents welcome a family affair to which they can bring their children. The movers and shakers of the community love the opportunity to politic and please the

21

*people with candies for their kids. The business owners come
out from their closets and into the streets to show their
prosperity and civic gratitude with signs like "Thank you for
letting us serve you." The cops are watching the parade at the
intersections. Traffic has been diverted from Main Street.*

*There were people I knew sitting on plastic and folding chairs
on the side walk, so I stopped to talk. There were people I
knew waving from the parade. There were people I knew
sitting on the grass slope in front of the senior citizen
apartments across the street. And there were a thousand
people I didn't know everywhere.*

*Regardless of the innumerable problems in the world, there is
no sign of discouragement here. Children abound. They are in
arms, in baskets, in strollers, in the street. They stand on the
trailers, wave from the fancy cars and steer the fire trucks.
The driver of the 1942 tractor couldn't have been more than
thirteen. (No license needed within three miles of the farm -
really! Right here in New Hampshire in the twenty-first
century.) The babies I knew are watching their children do
back flips on the street, line dance on a flat bed, or drive a
team of horses. (One big work horse trotted and his hooves
kicked out to the sides, like my mother's feet and hands did
when she ran.)*

*There are old people, too. The American Legion, the band
from Pittsfield, the Adeline singers, the original owner of a
forty-eight Ford ("Not for sale, one owner."), even a belly
dancer who had clearly been around for half a century or
more.*

But mostly in the parade were middle-aged drivers and vehicles; large vehicles, small ones, fast ones, old ones. The undertaker drives a status car. (License plate: 9TEEN 81 or WIFE N I) The farmers brought antiques - trucks, tractors, wagons. There was a double line of 24 Corvette Stingrays dated from 1956 to 2005, and a line of 36 old cars. (1981 and back are "classic" and 1961 and back are "antique.") There were fire vehicles ("We fight what you fear") and ambulances as far as you could see in both directions. (The AMBULANCE sign in front is written backwards.) They came from Newfield and Endfield and Montica Falls, ...from Emeryville (where's Emeryville?) and Vernon. Prissy rode on the back of a pickup truck / float, decorated with balloons and populated with a half dozen children, which advertised "cleaning and hauling almost anything."

There was a band new tractor/trailer, a four wheeler, a dune buggy, a 1943 tow truck (driven by Stan, one of the three McClintock brothers, a '52 John Deere tractor, and an old Ford Farmall tractor just like the one that Hunter and I learned to drive at Leipfreid's dairy farm. There was a '56 Chevy, red and white, like the one I ported goats in near Lexington, KY, except that this one was a convertible. (I took the back seat out to put the goats in.) There was a big wheeled bicycle from the century before last. Oh, but no motorcycles. They came to town last month. About a hundred of them.

So it would seem that we are a people who "Support Our Troops" and LUV our cars and trucks and motor homes, and ATVs, and maybe our kids, too. (The village chimes tolled seven as I walked up Spring Street on the way home. And it occurred to me that I was home.)

23

Luv tu yu all from me, Pete

==

In February 2006, Pete sent another update.

Update 27

*Tighten your britches and have another drink of orange juice.
Pete is going back to the oncology clinic in three weeks less a
day.*

*I went to the clinic today to talk to the doctor. He mentioned
bright spots at the spleen and in a lymph node in the left
clavicle area. He was referring to the CT scan back in May,
2005. ("Oh, I didn't know that." I said.) But in June and more
recently in November ... the CT scans were clean. But last
week's CT scan showed a hot spot, a recurrence at the spleen.*

*We did the scan because the blood work a couple of weeks
indicated an elevation of the CEA from 6.7 (normal range) to
32.0 (elevated), even while my blood counts and liver function
indicators were okay. Of course, I am symptom-less, and
fatter. Sarah (sister) said, "Don't worry about that. You might
need it." She loves me.*

*The doctor is reluctant to use a FOX (Oxiliplatin) regimen
because of the damage to the nerves in my extremities.
Instead, he recommends a FURI (I asked twice but still don't
remember: 5 FU +?) regimen, the one they used in June,
before terminating treatments. He said I seemed to have
tolerated it well. They have their treatments and insurance
pays. I cannot get confidence in alternative approaches.*

The clinic is busy. The earliest they could schedule me in was February 21. I still have the infusion port and the emergency cleanup kit for my car, so everything is ready. I could have received treatments in the hospital per se, this week, but I didn't want to adapt to a new team.

Work promises to be accommodating. I got the family leave paperwork so I can continue on a part-time basis without getting penalized for frequent absences. Like before, I will get the infusion started on one day and on the third day get disconnected from the infusion pump. Sessions every other week.

The psychosomatic effect of all this is an acute increase of sensation in my hands and feet. BP [blood pressure], pulse, respiration, and temp were all at or below my normals.

But this is not the only thing on my plate. Night before last a close friend and former fiancé of Willa's died unexpectedly. He was 43. There is much speculation about the cause of death. I advised Willa and others that, since there has been some history of heart disease (NOT to mention drugs and alcohol, smoking, and sedentary life style) that the politically correct finding would probably be "heart failure", without further details. Pat was a participant in the family autobody repair business, here in Medford, and was widely known. I expect there will be a large turnout for calling hours and services.

Janeane is coming from Tonawanda (without kids, I think). Karen expects to be home regardless.

Meanwhile, last Wednesday, we (Terrie and Jim and me) took Sonny to a new residence in Torrance called Renaissance Plaza. Sonny has talked to Terrie on the phone since and seems to be adapting okay. We all hope for the best. [Sonny, Pete's son, age about forty, was very ill with diabetes.]

I think that is it. Oh, I had a cold. A real nasal drip sort of thing. It started on Friday, but I worked extra on Saturday-Sunday, 3 PM to 3 AM. And then I was so stuffy on Sunday night that I kept snoring and snorting so that I woke myself up. .... I think it has been more than a decade since my last such illness ...

The nurse, Ruth, got a digital recording of the computer generated sounds of my song, Friday Night Awakening (Ruth's Song), which I scored using a digital music writer program.

===

Various family members and friends offered exercises, books, tapes, potions, alternate medical regimens, vitamins and magnetics of various kinds. Pete accepted everything graciously and ignored much of it. He tried some things – diet ideas, Zeolite, and the sodium bicarbonate wash of his abdomen, as described below.

However, other people's religious ideas were rejected out of hand, without discussion. Pete had explored ideas about God, redemption and the after-life during his hard years of struggle and loss, and he stood clear of most of it now. He didn't seem to want to talk about such issues now.

===

On February 18, 2006, Elinor wrote to him.

Hey, bro, I am very conscious that our sisters, Sarah and Caro, are visiting with you today, and I wish I were there! What a lot of miles between the east and west coast sometimes!

Are they coming to you because you are about to start (or just started) the new round of chemo? Drag!

Is this defined as a new outbreak or as a metastasis? Drag!

What is going to be different during this round, if anything?

Keep up your reports. You thought people would get bored or overwhelmed, but any one on your list who doesn't enjoy them just won't read them. People like me are reading every word/

Cheers……………….Elinor

And Pete answered:
Dear Ellilee, it is nice to hear from you. Our sisters may come up tomorrow [Sarah had a three hour drive and Caro six].. I don't know. I think Sare wants an excuse to talk to Caro without distractions. Free lunch, too.

I start a new round of chemo on Tuesday.

It is a metastasis. Who knows if it is new or recurrent. The doc said it was evident on the CT or MRI last spring. It is a drag. I think I am more nervous about it (this time) knowing something about what it entails.

It will be a little different in that there will be no Oxiliplatin which caused the distal neuropathy of which I am still continually aware. The new stuff is sometimes related to nausea, but I had two doses last June without any ...adverse effects.

Yeh, I'll write the updates when I have something to update.

Luv yu, too.

Pete

The dialogue continued.

Oh, darley,

I feel like acknowledging in a straight-forward way that this looks increasingly like a terminal ailment you are dealing with. But it's up to you to say what aspects of the experience you want to talk about, and with whom.
Of course, if it is, your updates are especially important, as they will become guide posts along the way we all will walk eventually. So far, you have been a great teacher.

So glad you visited me (along with the others) last December. I especially and constantly remember how you got up and started the coffee early.

Love you...............Elinor

Pete responded immediately.

Darley is good. That which assaults me is terminal 50% of the time. We will see. I have been dealing with it as such from the beginning.

Here is the disillusionment. The wisdom of the ages suggests that we should live as though we would die tomorrow. Given six months to live, we find that we cannot change who we are, what we have or how we live very much. ...

Our sisters are coming today, and I don't have any sherry. Sare said she was bringing food, but I didn't think to tell her to skip the food, we could get it here, but to bring the sherry, which we cannot get here on a Sunday.

Luv yu

Pete

Sarah wrote the next day to describe the visit.

How is Pete? Well, there are various answers to that question.

The first is, we had a lovely time, a visit to remember with a gentle smile. We got there at 10:15 Sunday morning, visited with his wonderful six-month old great granddaughter, made lunch, went off to Concord to sight-see, went to a play at Barkley University. Visited wonderful parks with lakes and gorges, went out to dinner, did some shopping and came home, visited, went to bed, got up at 6:30 and hit the road by 7am. Cold, bitter cold.

The second is, the only mention of the cancer was in the first three minutes after we arrived. He said that the general reaction to a metastasized cancer is that you have six months to live. This is not a prognosis but the general public's assumption. Pete said he was miffed when the doc told him he had seen the two other hot spots last May but didn't mention them. [But] the clavicle hot spot didn't show up on the last CT scan... He will start the chemo [again] tomorrow.

That was it, and any [little effort to get more was] met with a joke or a segue into something else. This morning he was up and out with no time for any goodlucks or keep in touch, just single focus on what was the next step in front of him, the bus route.

The third is my own subjective view. Pete looked good, ate well, enjoyed his food, handled the cold weather with a normal reaction, was good humored, had planned a wonderful day for the three of us, was very glad to have us come and was ready for us to leave. He controlled the conversation, enjoyed the humor and the opportunity to show us his city, and accommodated our need to ply him with books, tapes and vitamins. Below, a sadness held us all a little bit back....

He accepted the tapes from Millie [brother Hunter's wife] but declined my offer to do an acupressure treatment.

We saw the sweetest of Pete. We will see other aspects of him again, as we [have before].... His children see that quite a lot. Terrie is a darling and a saint whom Pete appreciates, but he can also be pretty hard on her.

There was no mention of so many [gone before] who swirled around – his kids and wife, our parents -- and for me still others who visited the conversations and glittered in the waterfalls and the hoarfrost in the valleys.

...The next six months are going to be tough, regardless of outcome. May we know what will be needed and when there is no need to do, may we just be.

Love, Sarah.

Elinor wrote back promptly:

Whee, I thought from Pete's remarks that you were just going for lunch! Glad you all had such fun together. Thanks for this in-depth report.

I, for one, assume Pete has a good bit more than six months to go, but it may not be any fun after 5-6 months. Or less. He is on my mind constantly, and so is the mortality of all of us. Not heavy, though; just processing and preparing.

I like your conclusion: When there is no need to do anything for Pete, let us just be.

Cheers..................Elinor

===

Pete sent another update a couple of weeks later, on March 12, 2006:

Update 28 (I think) –

...Today is a day of motivation and action. Last weekend we cut down the pear tree. We were going to prune it, but the ladder wouldn't reach the lowest branches and we remembered picking up the never-eaten fruit during the autumn. So, it came down.

Today the sun came out and the weather was warmer. Twenty degrees warmer. Jim [daughter Terrie's partner] We went out and actually got both the chain saw and the lawn mower started. I moved the pear tree across the lawn by tying it to the back of the mower and dragging it in low gear at about 1 mile per hour, over to the brush pile. The drag marks will be noticeable in the lawn until June.

Jim was going to use the chain saw, but he pulled the rope too far and jammed up the recoiler. While I got that straightened out, he took the ax to the apple tree. He got a good chunk out by the time I got the power saw working again. ... Then he worked at cutting across the trunk from the back. I was thinking that next time we refilled the gas tank [on the saw] we should tighten up the blade, but just then it came off the bar.

Well, Jim challenged me that he would get the tree down before I got the chain back on. He almost did. I got everything loosened up and then found that the chain blade was bent and would not go back on correctly.

[Some in the family wondered if these long stories about malfunctioning tools and equipment were metaphors for the condition of Pete's body?]

Well, Chip showed up with Alexis and their baby, [great granddaughter] Lucelia, interested in pizza. Chip and Jim succeeded in using my old five foot cross cut saw like a two man saw to finish cutting the apple tree down. It creaked and crackled and came down with a satisfying crash while I yelled "timber!"

Then we got the pizza and had supper at Terrie's. Jim had broken blisters on his hand. He'll be alright, tho'. Terrie's other daughter Lisa and her boyfriend are visiting for an overnight. Chip and Alexis took their kid home.

So, I just completed the second session of my second regimen of chemo. My hand and feet are prickly again and my nose runs. I didn't have enough morning sickness this time to throw up.

But the dreams are wild. I didn't know whether to wake up with the prospect of throwing up or to continue sleeping, dreaming of fighting in the insurrection. One dream: I was driving the bus…As I was going along, I began to notice that the steering was sticking every now and then. When the steering got tight, I began to realize that the brakes didn't work as well as usual. This caused me enough concern to call dispatch on the two-way radio and ask for the shop. The mechanic got on the radio and asked what my problem was. I explained as well as I could and finished by saying that "I have a bus that doesn't steer and has no brakes." [Speaking of metaphors!]

Well, he asked me for my location and my bus number. I told him I was at Court Street and Church. He said, "Where?!"

33

As I thought about it, I realized that I was in Marsdale, not Concord. I don't drive a bus in Marsdale. So I answered him by saying, "Disregard. 505 clear." The number was scrawled in chalk up above the cab, which looked like the inside of an old steam engine. Then I turned my head towards my passengers, saying, "This is a dream. You're going to have to get off here." Before waking up, I heard one customer complaining to another, "What does he mean this bus won't steer and won't stop? Does he want us to get off a moving bus?"

Okay, okay, subtly humorous, not very exciting. It was very vivid. I made an effort to remember and to tell it for you. …

Sarah came up and tried to treat me with a variety of alternative methods. The chemo makes me feel yucky anyway. But I am still eating and doing, so maybe…
Caro [younger sister] came, too. She makes my plants happy. She makes me happy, too. I thought Kathy [niece] was going to show, but hers was just a disappointing no-show. Kathy, you can come any time.

For you medical types, I am not getting the Oxalplatin stuff this time. I am getting Camptosar …along with Avistin, Leucovorin, and 5FU. I think maybe they use the worst first so that subsequent sessions are not so bad, but I didn't ask. I did ask about vitamins and learned that C and E are anti-oxidants that may help to prevent cancer, but interfere in the action of the 5FU. The leucovorin is "like a partial vitamin B," said the technician who prepared the concoction used in my infusion pump. Vitamin D is good for metabolizing calcium, but with milk and a complete diet and a one-a-day vitamin, I should be getting enough.

34

That's it for now. Replay with your questions and concerns.

Luv yu all and all of yurs.

Pete

People didn't realize it at the time, but later, googling Pete's name, they found that he wrote an article about cancer from a patient's perspective which was included in a news blog called Health Supreme in July 2006.

He sent another update to the family. Here is part of it.

As we were wrapping up our conversation, I said to the doctor, "I wish we were talking about someone else." He said, "I wish we weren't talking about anyone."

We were talking after having spent a lot of time looking at the Computer Tomography (CT or CAT) scans from last week and from May 2006. In the top left hand corner of the computer screen was a full torso x-ray image of me, for reference. Below was the CT from last week on the left and on the right was the scan from May. Using the mouse, the doctor could manipulate the images so that the two on the bottom of the screen showed the same transverse section of my abdomen and scrolled up or down together. (Oh, the wonders of modern technology!)

There, the doctor pointed (click, click), was my spleen, with the small (12-14 mm) mass, in both images. It had not changed much in the last two and a half months.

Over here (click, click) was my kidney and right here (zoom...) is the dark spot that seems to be a benign cyst.

Now you see this dark area around the perimeter of the spleen in last week's CT, it is fluid under the membrane around the organ. And over here is your pancreas with a similar dark area. (This isn't seen in the May CT.) The fluid is probably coming from this area here (click, click) where the connecting tissue is thickened. This is what concerns me, says the doc. He explains that the thickened area in the abdominal tissue is probably tumorous and inflamed and seeping fluid into the abdominal membranes that is then "puddling" around the pancreas and spleen. The fluid probably comes from cancerous cells.

With the nurse, we scheduled the resumption of chemo for Tuesday this week. Chemo will continue until side effects become too debilitating. Then we will take another break. And then...?

[Pete gave little updates about four of his children and then said], today Alexis is throwing a birthday party for my great grand-daughter, Lucelia ... who will be one year old on July 25. Lucelia wandered into my (half of the house) the other day and called out, "Gra-pa" as clear as could be. ...

Luv yu and all yurs,

Pete

Holly, his youngest sister, living near Boston, found this letter frustrating:

.... I kind of want to shriek at you!! What does this description (click, click) of your visit to the doctor MEAN? What is the diagnosis? More importantly, what is the prognosis? What are you telling us REALLY? Because what you told us ACTUALLY is USELESS. What is going on with you? You sort of disappeared for a while. So what's happening?

Pete answered immediately.

Dear Holly and other people who love me,

Your fears are justified. The cancer has metastasized and is now growing in the connective tissues in my abdomen and spreading to my vital organs. I am going to resume chemo in order to slow its growth but the outlook is grim. The timing is uncertain. Who knows? Six months or six years?

I am here. My denial is functioning well. I waste a lot of time with distractions. Family is engaging. I am changed and unfamiliar to myself. I feel much better physically, having been off chemo for six weeks. I feel anxious and disappointed at going back on chemo. It is not easy having a potentially fatal disease that seems to be gaining ground in spite of debilitating poison. But then again, it is not hard, there not being any more that I can do about it than what I am doing. The harder part is that family and friends are no better at dealing with realities they cannot affect. Does my news and condition impinge unfairly on them? It is what it is. Unfair,

37

unexpected, unpleasant. So I sound nonchalant. The facts, ma'am, just the facts. I am sorry, too.

... Maybe you should call me up. I am home most of the time. I talked to Sarah for nearly an hour the other day. Or send an e-mail with a time and number for me to call you.

There is nothing that is mysterious about my situation. When I relate what I see, hear and say, I expect that you all will understand it the way I do. ... I want to scream, too, but I, too, realize that it will not help. I do what I can and leave the rest. I do what I can and expect the best. I'm sorry, too. Then I keep on keeping on. I learn and experience and share from my new wisdom. Come on, enjoy the trip, suffer the effort, experience the extremes, risk it all. Remember, every life is terminal.

Only long afterwards did they realize that with this statement and others like it to individuals, Pete saved the whole extended family from the agony of secrecy, dishonesty and denial about his cancer and his immanent death.

Elinor wrote in response, with copies to all.

Dear good tough realist brother, how I love you and all your/our family people! Thanks for putting it all in a new set of words. We will need to hear it in various ways as the weeks go by probably, because we don't want you to have a terminal illness, and we don't like knowing that we are in line behind you. And of course we are mad at the messenger – you! Even though it is just the ordinary facts you are telling us.

Now say more about a work party at your house in Medford…

Cheers……………….Elinor

===

No full-fledged work party at Medford developed, but some siblings went to help Pete sort papers and photographs. Meanwhile, Pete got interested in trying treatments of Zeolite, which promised to take the heavy metals out of his system. There were no insurance benefits. Brother Hunter took the lead in organizing family support for this medication with a letter on October 16, 2006

Sarah et al –

The sibs and [family friend] Rob E. have come through in fine fashion and we are now ready to order a full initial supply of Zeolite for the second month's use….I will order eight bottles of Zeolite today and sign Pete up for an ongoing prescription if he confirms.

The cost of the first order will be $310. (That's two four-packs at $140 each and a $30 membership.) The next order will be placed on or about November 30 and will be $280, as will be the ongoing orders [in December, February, April and so forth]. If you could send me your check on or about the first of each purchase month … then I would be able to place a timely order. … Your contribution amount (subject to your confirmation) is $81.40 now, then $73.15 each purchase month hereafter. Please let me know if this seems doable.

Many thanks and much love,

Hunter

Pete agreed to this plan and his five siblings and one friend contributed to cover the cost of the Zeolite for six or eight months before it was discontinued.

===

Pete and Elinor talked some on the phone on October 15, 2006, a day of nausea and diarrhea and sleeplessness for him. She wrote the next day.

Hey, good morning, Pete, after seventeen hours of misery yesterday, I should hope you slept well last night.

I took a turn lying awake a long time, trying to imagine all the things you are dealing with. It is all very interesting to me, despite the distressing parts -- the final major challenge of life. I know it all from books and from a certain limited professional angle, but you are the one with the extensive personal experiences of death. I would be glad to hear as much as you want to tell.

The only item we really dealt with on the phone yesterday is the topic of adding alternative remedies into the mix. Everything else you said had another silent paragraph or whole chapter behind it. The misery of constant diarrhea. The worn vocal cords from vomiting. The inability to eat. The risks of driving yourself to the doctor. The evasive daughter. The mess in the house. Your resentment of the

pharmaceutical system. Being too tired and sick to deal with
Sonny [his sick son] *or the bills. The cost of this care. Your*
continuing engagement in the political world.

Yikes, even when you can only lie there, you have tons to think
about, when you are able to think at all. How the future might
play out. How this all effects your relations with your
children. With your siblings, neighbors, colleagues. Your
God? There are things you want to get done, things you no
longer have time for, things that make you fed up, things you
hate to think of losing.

I imagine your mood shifting constantly from indifference to
irritation to mourning to anger to determination and back to
indifference.

Well, don't let me go on -- suffice it to say that I have been
thinking about it all a good deal and am up for conversations
when and if you are. Your temperament is so different from
mine that it strains my brain to imagine how all this goes for
you. And my experience is so limited, that I am strained
again to imagine how it would be for me.

Let's talk whenever the time is right.

Cheers......................Elinor

Pete responded with the "tool box" letter, copied to all, which
later became well known throughout the family.

Dear Ellilee,

It may be better to write. Talking allows little time for

41

reflection.

I have a tool box. In my tool box are useful tools for various situations. Among these tools you can find "The Virtue of Selfishness". I don't remember the author, except that she is a woman. Very useful when it comes to doing what is important to me. Also you can find "I'm Okay, you're Okay". This is about "transactional analysis", the patterns of family relationships, internalized roles of parent / child / ego. It has been very useful in fixing or at least understanding people's perspectives. The Twelve Steps program has 12 very useful tools. They are not only applicable to addictive behaviors, but can be applied to all sorts of experiential situations. For example "Take the best, leave the rest" allows for a non-critical, non-combative response/reaction to other people. Similarly, "Live and let live" permits one to tolerate other perspectives and behaviors. "One day at a time." "Let go and let God." You get my drift. There are many tools from the Sermon on the Mount. And a special tool comes from Thomas Jefferson's rendition of the New Testament, looking at Jesus, the man and his message.

It also helps to have adopted the turn of mind familiar to you in our father. It is a hierarchy of placidity, tolerance, determination and decisiveness. There are, of course, many detailed ingredients mixed in.

I have learned much from both spiritual and scientific thinking. These have contributed important tools to my collection. I continue to be an avid reader of the Scientific American. Although I remember few details, I have learned about intricate patterns that overlap and intersect and change in interactions. Meanwhile, Sarah has informed me of Native

American thinking and tribal and cultural norms that exist that are diametrically opposed to our cultural norms but are similar to the teachings of Jesus. Sometimes it seems a shame that I cannot pass most of this useful information on but then I recollect and recall that I pass bits and pieces on everyday. Viz, this.

And now, today, the bills are paid, the floor has been mopped, the symptoms have been out to the post office and town offices. People know that I am still alive. They also know that I am a marked man. (Dead man, walking.)

My mood doesn't change much, just the tools I am using at the moment. I do have feelings, but they aren't much good for informing action.

You say you want to hear as much as I want to tell. It seems that you have. What more do you desire? I am a bore for details because I do not dwell on them. My past is quickly foggy. I live in the day and for the next day.

Now do you want me to call?

Luv yu, luv yours,

Pete

==

All during the spring and summer, Pete and his family had been much concerned about their son and brother, Sonny, who was terminally ill with complications of diabetes and residing in a nursing home. Monitoring Sonny's care focused Pete's energy and attention. Terrie was extensively involved in the care of her brother, too. Finally Sonny's years of disability and illness came to an end. Arranging his funeral in November 2006 was a major project. Sonny was hardly more than forty years old. Would Pete fade away after this last generous effort?

But he had other projects to complete.

At some point around about Christmas time, 2006, Pete let the family know, in a low key sort of way, that he had sued the primary physician who misdiagnosed his symptoms for months at the beginning of this saga. Pete had been astute in his collection of documentation, his selection of a malpractice lawyer, and his insistence upon adequate recompense for "losing twenty years of his life." He won the suit and was awarded a large amount of money. He would never say how much, but they think it was near half a million dollars. He paid off his debts, gave generously to his children, and even dreamed of some major travels. After a life time of near poverty, this success improved his outlook and perhaps his health for many weeks.

===

There were no decisive changes in Pete's condition in the next six months. He continued to suffer through the chemotherapy, work part-time, and live with the distractions, joys and problems of his big family. He sent an update on April 11, 2007, to the whole extended family and related friends.

Update April 2007

Dear All:

*I missed my appointment with Susan, the nurse practitioner
(NP) on Monday this week. (But she took me today, Tuesday.)
...At 4 pm, I was at the clinic looking for an article on page
64 in the magazine when Susan showed up, ready to go. I got
measured (fat and hypertensive) and we began to talk.*

*"No, nothing in particular, Susan. Chemo is like a syndrome:
everything is just a little worse and I haven't had time to fully
recuperate since the last session."*

*NP: Well, maybe we could just do every three weeks from now
on.*
*Me: Well maybe, but I remember Dr. S. saying last year that
the two-week schedule was because of the way the cancerous
cells replicated.*
NP: Yes, but more than two weeks apart is OK.
*Me: Oh, talking of two years ago, Dr. S. had some graphs of
the probabilities, you know, the numbers.*
*NP: Yes, Dr. S is better at the numbers. Why don't we have
him come in and explain that for you.*
*Me: (with a smile and raised eyebrows) Oh, we could do
that?)*
*Dr.S.: I can draw you a graph. (After extensive rummaging
around in the cupboards and drawers, he selects a 4x4 gauze
in its wrapper.)*

*I can't replicate the graph here (thank goodness) but the gist
of it is that half the patients diagnosed with metastatic (stage
IV) colorectal cancer have died, are dying or will die at
around 24 months. About half of those still alive will stay
alive thru 60 months. Dr. S. has a patient who is colon-
cancer free after three years of treatment, almost ten years*

45

now. Susan observes that I have no disease symptoms at this time. This is a good thing. Both agree that I am in good shape. Treatment at this time has become an individual thing. We just carry on, carrying on.

So, here is what we need to do: find out how to carry on. The surgery and the clinic treatments have been "successful" to date. I am done with surgery. Now, how do we get me beyond the treatments? Extending the interval between treatments is a good first step. (It really messes up my schedule, tho.) Part of the concern I have is that the treatments are keeping the cancerous cells at bay, but are debilitating the body. If we discontinue treatments, the body is less prepared to contend with the cell growth. We need a plan to maximize bodily recuperation, regeneration and resistance to cancerous cells. And we need to do this with feet on the ground and eyes wide open.

So, for now, send information, not remedies. Send contact information for those who have been able to win some acclamation in this area of expertise. I am a difficult and skeptical patient. I want to know and I will ask. I need to be convinced. When Susan mentioned my elevated (164/92) blood pressure, I asked what that was about. She acknowledged that Leucovorin (one of the poisons I get) could be causing a higher blood pressure. She said "we can treat it, but you would have to take the medicine, not just the prescription." I am resistant to taking medicines to treat the effect of other medicines. I know it is the American way. I know that it is very profitable to some people with stocks in the pharmaceutical industries. But I suspect that there is a better (and cheaper) way for me to go.

So, that is the way it is. I hope we can make it better.

Luv tu yu and all of yurs from me, Pete

==

Meanwhile, there was the question of "Penny Lake" in the background. Pete and his siblings had inherited a tiny cottage on a fraction of an acre that fronts on a pristine little New Hampshire lake. The county reassessed the area, looking for enhanced property tax revenues. The rustic little cabin was assessed at $14,000, the prime lake-front property at $230,000! The property taxes suddenly became hard for the family to afford.

Pete came up with a proposal to establish an endowment whose interest earnings would cover the operating costs of the cabin. Family people found it hard to understand by e-mail. An enterprising niece organized a wonderful weekend work party at the cabin, thus providing an occasion where Pete could explain and many family members could discuss the proposal.

The details were complicated and in the end, many months after Pete's death, they shifted to another plan. The real impact of the weekend, though, was that Pete was, for the first time in family memory, the one that had money and a clever financial plan to offer. He also initiated a process that would keep the whole extended family talking and working together far on into the future. Everyone remained discreet about how this was Pete's swan-song, the last gracious gift he had to offer them.

Pete's Progress

Chapter 2: Slow Surrender

Several weeks later, Pete reported again on his health status, with a recap of the previous four months.

Update July 2007

April 19, I had kemo. [Why did he stop spelling it "chemo"?] I was acutely ill for four days and still recuperating after 14 days. When I went in for the treatments, I suggested (it was a suggestion; I talk with my medical staff as tho I was a consultant on my case) that we should skip the next treatment and then schedule treatments for every three weeks, rather than every two weeks as we had been doing since the beginning. After that discussion and a visit with the Doctor, later, we all decided that we could do a complete re-evaluation, including complete blood tests and a CT scan before resuming treatments. The adjustments to the schedule then put us into July.

I went to Karen's graduation one day in May and to her Commissioning [into the Air Force] another day.   I went to Washington, DC for my national union conference the last week of May and then to Penny Lake for the work weekend. (See Update May, 2007) We did half of [daughter] Willa's roof in early June and the second half two weeks later. I went to a high school graduation party, too. And I got a motorcycle in there somewhere and spent many hours on the road. Then, in July, I went to Sarah's (post hip surgery, hers) and from there I visited with Hunter's doctor friend, in Philadelphia. ...

When I got home from PA, I was very bloated. I called the oncology clinic on Sunday and left a message, but I had to wait until Friday after the CT scan, to get a paracentesis (para-sen-tee-sis = insert a needle into the abdomen and let the fluid drain) done by Dr S., in the oncology suite in the hospital. We drained off about 3.5 L of fluid (about a gallon). Salt is a "no no." when getting fluid, but the muscles in the legs cramp without it.

We got the CT scan done on July 19, with a belly full of fluid.

Meanwhile, I wondered if the fluid was related to the NCD (zeolite) or to a long respite from kemo. I had been off kemo for three months, by then.

Last weekend, Alexis had a big birthday party for Lucelia (b. 07/25/07) in the back yard (the weather was perfect) here. Then on Tuesday I talked to Dr. S. about the results of all the testing.

The blood work was OK, my red and white cell counts were fine and there was no indication of liver problems. The CEA was up, from about 115 the previous three times while

49

doing treatments, to 187. So, the number probably does not reflect the rapid regrowth of normal cells after kemo. The CEA is quite specific to antibodies produced by cancerous cells. Either the cells are producing more antibodies, more rapidly, or there are more cells producing the anti-bodies. Either way...

The CT scan showed lots of fluid. There were no "hot spots" on my liver or pancreas or lymph nodes, but suspicious spots on my lung tissue were now a little larger than they had been. That is not conclusive proof of involvement, but certainly suggests unusual growth. The peritoneum, the connective and supporting tissues in my abdomen, showed more extensive thickening than in the previous scans. This is probably related to the ascites (as-sí-tees = abdominal fluid), which had begun to appear about 5 months ago. Like burned skin, the tissue is inflamed and seeps fluid, like pus.

So, doc, I said, if I had just been sent in because of the CT scan and the ascites, and you were seeing me for the first time, how would you treat me?

We talked about 5FU and the other chemicals that I had last year. We talked about newer adjuncts and how we can use one or another but not both, because they have not been tested for compatibility.

When the nurse from the treatment suite called me up, she asked if Wednesday (this week) would be okay. I said, sure. At 1:00 PM, for a finger prick and then infusion until 5:00 PM? Yes, I said. And back to unhook on Friday at 3:00? What?! I exclaimed, Do you mean the pump and everything? Well, yes, she said, meekly. Doctor ordered it. (Me and my big mouth!) Well, eventually I agreed.

I saw the doctor on Friday morning for my second paracentesis (a little over 4 L, about 8 ½ pounds and five inches off my girth) Doc, I said, I think this will be alright, but its getting hard to be objective as a consultant while being subjective as a patient so I'm leaving it up to you. Take good care of me.

Oh, he said as he processed what I had said, okay. And then we proceeded with the paracentesis.

So, it seems I will remain on the inexorable spiral down. Treatments, side effects, reprieves, and around again. But I have plenty to do on the good days.

Friday evening a skinnier me dressed in a tuxedo gave Willa away (again) in her wedding dress (white with sparkles) to Cliff (in tux) at the Run River Inn ... The weather was seasonal, with a fierce thunderstorm with lightening that shut the electricity off for a couple of hours prior to the ceremony and hit the big pine tree next to the Inn. Dinner was good and the in-laws are nice (from Oklahoma). My toast to the bride and groom was well received and there were no major catastrophes.

Back to normal (?)...

Wish me well.

A few days later, another update, including another wedding, long anticipated.

Update Sept 07

Regarding my visit with my oncologist yesterday: Just as expected. No definitive answers. Just things are the way they are. Even the fluid can stay for a while. No expressed concern about the cancer. No chance that Dr will use anything not sanctified by the PTB (powers that be), FDA, CRI, NIH, AMA....

So I said to the doctor, you might as well tell me about that snake oil, 'cause you know I am going to go home and look it up anyway.

And the doctor asked, "What sort of 'snake oil?'" I talked about the wedding while I collected my thoughts and said, seamlessly, "The snake oil you asked about is Essiac." So doc gave me a brief history of Essiac and said it wouldn't hurt me, leaving a hint of approval for its use.

I suggested that I liked the alternate paradigm for cancer genesis: cell infection rather than cell mutation. But Dr. S. answered every question with years of experience and knowledge, and I do not have the information at hand to even explain that there is a difference between virus damaged cells (paploma, for example) that become targets for invasion and virus infected cells. ... Dr.S. brought up the case of virus infected cells in animals (bovine leukemia). So I went home and looked it up and sent him the abstract of a study to determine if bovine leukemia virus could be the cause of some breast cancers. (I noted that it seemed incongruent with the huge volume of knowledge about breast cancer that its causes were not known or that infection with a sub-cellular life form had not been ruled out long ago). Dr. S. is a very nice man. He is very smart, very well educated and very tolerant.

Meanwhile, I am very fat with fluid. I seem to be growing to accommodate the load. However, either I am losing weight off the rest of me, or the fluid level really is quite stable.

Last night Alexis assisted me with an injection.

Friday night, before Karen's wedding, one of the Collins clan assisted. [That's the groom's family] The Collins family turned out in total for the wedding. I walked along the hotel corridor and encountered friendly people I had not seen in decades, and several small people I had never seen before but whose faces seemed familiar, at every door. Weddings are such beautiful occasions for family gatherings.

The wedding was wonderful, light- hearted and fun. There were enough minor glitches right along to make it interesting. The weather was terrific (for central NH, as Karen explained), sunny and breezy.

Karen, UPS keeps showing up with boxes for you.

I got the tux back on time.

Luv tu all,

Pete

===

Seeing his youngest daughter married had been a major item on Pete's last TO DO list. Now he was content with his family, despite its difficult history. But he would often, during this period, express strong hostility towards the medical establishment and the pharmaceutical companies. Perhaps they were a more tangible enemy that the cancer itself.

Pete was still riding around the countryside on his motorcycle. Some wondered if he would crash it, sort of by accident, and one sister asked him. "I thought about it," he admitted, "but it would make too much of a mess." Finally one day, when the bike fell over, he was too weak to lift it himself, so he gave it up.

Many of the East Coast family members met at Sarah's for Thanksgiving. The shared festivities included testimonials and poems offered for Pete. The talk behind the scenes included concerns that he needed more help at home.

In Arizona, Elinor began to wonder if she should go across the country to be with him. Newly retired amd living alone, she was responsible for no one at home and wanted to see snow falling again after so many years. But would her sisters or Pete's daughters feel that she was usurping their role, taking their place? Even if they did, though, they were all working, or had children or partners. Still very unsure, she began asking people if they thought she should come.
She exchanged short e-messages around December 6 with Pete's daughter, Janeane.

Janeane: *When are you thinking of coming to Medford?*

Elinor: *Well, if people like the idea, I was thinking I would come when Pete can no longer drive at all. I have already started preparing for coverage of my tasks here ... but I got the impression from Pete that it wouldn't be necessary until after Christmas or later. I would fly into Concord, right? I need to start researching flights.*

Janeane: *I feel that Pop needs some additional attention right now, so those of us in the area will have to work together ... to get those things covered. We need to cover grocery shopping and meal planning etc.*

Elinor: *OK, Janeane, I will start thinking in terms of coming earlier than later. Are you saying that Pete is not shopping or cooking even now? Is he driving at all? I'll talk to him again. I know he will be in Philadelphia much of next week.*

Janeane: *He doesn't like talking about it, so it's hard to get accurate information. But he sort of blew up at Alexis the other day, saying that she wasn't reliable ... she probably didn't even know he was counting on her to provide a hot meal. He was talking to me about calling Meals on Wheels and getting ... a home health aide or something like that. I asked if he wouldn't prefer family and he said, "Naw, people are only strangers for a couple of days and then you get to know them." ... But it puts the rest of the family in a predicament because half of them think he is still OK and don't recognize the need. And when I try to tell them, they think I am exaggerating. ...Holly [Pete's youngest sister] is coming on Monday and will be there through Friday or Saturday ... so next week is covered. Personally, I am just waiting to hear back after they [return from Philadelphia to*

55

*hear] what the outcome is. If they think it's just weeks, then
I will probably start looking into taking a leave from work.*

She also wrote to Alexis, the granddaughter who lives in the
other half of Pete's duplex.

*Hi, Alexis, your Gran-Pop and I had a good phone talk
yesterday. One idea came up that we both liked, but he said
I should run it by you.*

*We are thinking that if Pete gets so that he cannot drive
himself, even around town, I could come east and stay with
you all for a while. I know you have gone back to work and
have got a lot of responsibility, as well as being pregnant
again. Also, Pete probably shouldn't be alone during the
day any more.*

*I am semi-retired and have no one at home to care for. I am
working on a couple of projects that can be done from
anywhere as long as I have a computer. You've got a nice
little extra room upstairs. So it might all work easily.*

What do you think?

Cheers.........................Elinor

*Hey, Aunt Elinor, sorry it took me so long to reply, I have
been busy. It sure would be nice to have a little help around
the house and with Grandpa. It's up to you guys. Sounds
good to me. Love Ya –Alexis*

======================================

56

Meanwhile, there was still a trip to Philadelphia planned. Pete had been seeing doctors at the Cancer Treatment Center of America there for several months during the summer and fall, staying with brother Hunter and his wife, Millie. CTCA had set him up with a port into his belly which allowed for a frequent "wash" of his abdominal cavity with bicarbonate soda. Granddaughter Alexis was administering the wash at home every few days, but Pete drove to Philadelphia once a month or so to check everything out with the CTCA. By December, it no longer seemed prudent for him to make the trip alone, so Holly flew up from Boston to accompany him. On December 17, she reported to the whole family distribution list.

Hi All,

I've talked with several of you already and this will be repetitious, but here's the scoop:

Last Tuesday I flew to Concord with connection at JFK with NO DELAYS!! I returned to Boston on Saturday with connection at Washington - Dulles with NO DELAYS!! The first huge blizzard in the Boston area hit on Thursday while I was gone ... The other arrived just after I did. Unbelievable good fortune!

.... On Wednesday Pete and I had a leisurely time revving our engines for the day and didn't get on the road for real (ie, after gas station, bank, bakery, water purchase...) until almost 2. Thereafter it was an uneventful 4-1/2 hour drive to Hunter and Millie's house. Pete slept part of the way. ...At Hunter's, he went to his room at 8ish and watched a little TV before going to sleep. ...

The Cancer Treatment Center of America (CTCA): Pete and I went on Thursday noonish to the CTCA. ... They sent us off to get the lab work, chest x-ray, and lunch with a pager in-hand. At 2:30 (I think) we went into the examining room to see the doctor. ...

In the opening Q&A, I learned that Pete has had tingling in his feet and hands for 3 years, but it is not as bad now as it once was. He has also had swelling in both hands and feet but said there was less of that in the last week. He suffers from weakness and fatigue. He didn't like the term "shortness of breath", but said he struggled with "labored breathing". He said that he drains one liter of fluid every other day from his very distended belly. When asked how he was mentally, he said, "EXCELLENT!"

Pete has 2 holes in his body more than those with which he was born ...

[These were the two ports, one in his chest for chemo and one in his abdomen for flushing out fluids produced by the cancer. Holly provided a lot of detail about the treatments, and said "nothing seems to help." She relayed extensive discussion with the doctor about Pete's lungs. Then she and Pete went back to Hunter and Millie's.]

Pete said ... that Dr. B. was far more approachable and conversant this time than on previous visits. I found the doctor to be gentle and kind and tolerant but not very informative. I asked for him to call me and talk privately. Pete signed authorization for same. But even when I asked him directly for some sort of timetable based on his experience, he said he "never makes predictions." They are always wrong. It also depends a lot on what treatments

Pete agrees to have. "You will know when he is a lot sicker and needs your help."

The Home Scene: Alexis, Chip and baby Lucelia live in "the other apartment" in Pete's house. There is no door that separates the two living spaces, though. Perhaps Pete seldom goes into their apartment, but they enter the house from outdoors through his outside door. There is a lot of coming and going between the two. They share one dishwasher. Alexis loads and unloads the dishwasher and puts away the dishes. Chip and Alexis put up and decorated the Christmas tree in Pete's living/dining room. They sweep up the dropped needles. They deal with his trash and recycling. When the forecast was for snow they put his car in the barn. They deal with shoveling and driveway plowing. They bring in the mail unless he goes out for some other reason. ...

And more important than any of the above, they provide a very calm, generous, helpful, loving, smiley atmosphere. Both Alexis and Chip are quiet sorts (not incessant talkers like the Bowers family). As Pete put it, "Chip will always do whatever he is asked. He doesn't know how to say no." He is good to Pete that way, but also to Alexis.

Alexis, for her part, is gentle and warm and self-effacing, and, "Oh, I don't mind Grandpa's grumbling. I really look up to him."

Lucelia is 2-1/2. Need I say more?! She is a sweetheart. She chatters away in a language which even her mother doesn't always understand! She is shy but very cute. She has a totally contagious giggle which makes everybody smile.

Pete could not have it better and he knows it. He even says it out loud!!

Let's see. What else? I am unclear about the status of Pete's paperwork. He tells me that he has a DNR in place [do not resuscitate order]. He has a will "with four or five executors." ?? Ahem. I don't know if anybody has copies of these papers which would confirm all this. That should probably be attended to by somebody soon.

Aside from the paperwork, there's an issue about meals. Pete's kids have stocked his refrigerator with food: some easy microwaveable frozen meals, salads in a bag, milk, eggs, potatoes, nuts, dried fruit... We didn't have to get groceries while I was there. But it became clear that Pete is not inclined to cook for himself when he is alone. ..."What's the point?" ...It's too much like work for him to even think of preparing the meal. ... He was happy to have somebody place a plate of food in front of him, but he doesn't eat much. It seems that the pressure in his abdomen is upon his stomach, too. He has no capacity. He is full in no time, but is then hungry again before too awfully long.
Pete's affect is deceiving. He comes across as better than he feels, I think. He needs to lie down and even to sleep often. But when he is up, he doesn't seem real sick. He may seem grumpy (in a mostly good-natured sort of way), but not sick. ...He's slow to ask for help. He's only too happy to receive it, though. I would hope that everybody who visits him would remember this.

I guess that's everything I can think of except to say that I had a totally wonderful time with Pete. We talked about LOTS of stuff. He is a really good person with a lot of wisdom in many areas. I was really glad I went.

Pete's next appointment at CTCA is on Tuesday, January 15. He should be there by 12:00 for lab work, x-ray and lunch. Who will volunteer to drive him from Medford to Philly?

Love,
Holly

It was that last paragraph that decided Elinor on going to New Hampshire from Arizona on January 12, in order to drive Pete to Philadelphia again. But at some point, the idea of another treatment at CTCA was abandoned, and the purpose of the trip shifted. Pete was going to need a care giver at home until he reached the end of the road.

She wrote to Sarah about this.

The kids (sic: Pete's grown children) will know that my coming means that Pete is near the end of the road. I'll be "the messenger" and they will resent it, probably subconsciously. Shucks. I am going to name an end date for my visit, March 15, and mention that Caro and Janeane are willing to spend time with Pete after that, so that no one feels we are rushing him off.

After Christmas Day, as so often happens with ill people, Pete's energy and intention seemed to flag, and there was a bit of anxiety about whether January 12 would be too late. Janeane arranged for a work leave from her job, and stayed with him from January 2 until her aunt got there on January 12.

61

Hearing of the trip she planned, many of Elinor's friends said they were praying for Pete, even people in Arizona who didn't know him from Adam. She was impressed and told him about it in an e-mail, but he only harrumphed in reply.

Before going, she sent another message to her sister Caro.

Caro, I was perplexed in retrospect by my own statement to you on the phone that I was not particularly experienced with "these matters" -- death and dying. Why did I say that?

I am glad you asked, because it made me ponder. Of course, you were right. Since it was all part of my work running adult day health programs for so long, I am extensively experienced with old age, physical disability, and dementia; with the rules, service programs, and funding sources; with the literature. I have given much attention to the meaning of mortality for how I live my life, to the after-life possibilities, to related theological issues. I "practice dying" as a spiritual exercise. I have attended several deaths and have helped to prevent three suicides. I am a knowledgeable advocate of legal euthanasia.

But at the moment you asked, I was preoccupied with the immanent death of a sibling. That's new to me. Maybe those of you who were close to Seb [our foster brother] when he died know more than I do about this one.

On the day you asked, I was grieving the loss to Pete (and some future day to myself) of the beauties of this complex planet. This gorgeous tree, that scintillating line of music......I remember this kind of mourning when Father died. I didn't listen to "his" Mahler symphony for two or

62

three years after his death. I couldn't bear to think that he had "lost" this music. This is the bit I must still grapple with, the letting go of earthly delights.

Pete says that he spends much of his time "playing poker" on his computer. Maybe he is already weaning himself from the delights (except for Lucelia!).

Thanks for bringing these ideas into focus for me.

Cheers…………Elinor

Pete's Progress,

Chapter 3: The care-giving routine

During this stage, Caro, in New York City, talked to Elinor by phone and then sent the first message that went to many family members and friends.

January 13, 2008

The guard has changed. Janeane, after an efficient, productive, and loving week at Pete's, has now gone back to her family in Sharon. Elinor arrived in Medford from San Fran last night, via Concord, and has now caught up on her jet lag.

Armed with tons of handover information from Janeane, Elinor is now settling in with Pete as they try, together, to figure out the reconfiguration of his internet and her wi-fi.

If they succeed, Elinor will update us all by email every few days, whenever there is news. If they don't, she will communicate the news once a day or so to me, and I will send out an update.

Thanks to everyone for their love, concern, prayers, and thoughts.

Best wishes for the coming week. Caro

Elinor started her reports to Pete's long list of friends and family the next day. There were about thirty on the list at this point. Many of their responses are included below. There were also many phone conversations and visits. Everyone was contributing whatever he or she could.

Pete's Progress, January 14

Hi, guys, Pete and I are figuring out pretty well how to get along with one another, the hospice people, the weather and the damned disease.

It's all OK except for the last. A zig-zag course: good day, bad day; good hour, bad hour. Pete slept OK and woke up feeling OK, then suddenly was overcome with retching. Recovered from that and felt OK midday, then suddenly had dreadful abdominal cramps.

Hospice nurse (male) came, is helpful, but it takes time to get MD OK for changed prescriptions.

The room monitor and call system and wireless Internet all seem to be working OK now. I have a nice room, good bed, found the library and saw snow falling. :)

Tomorrow we go to Concord to drain the pleural cavity, although low fluid intake has meant that issue is not pressing right now as once feared.

Cheers...............Elinor

She exchanged ideas with Sarah, too. Sarah wrote first.

Ellie, twenty four hours, so you have seen the best and the worst, I would guess.

How do you find it? Did folks come around to say hello? Are you recovered from your jet lag? Has Pete started drinking water, with the promise of drainage of the pleural cavity?

Collecting info is the name of the game for you for another day or two. Janeane said she was counting on laying out everything for you. I think she needed to pass the baton and be free of a tough, tough week. Pete confessed to me last night that he had gotten pretty miffed with Janeane. Having others take control is tough.

I hope you will send us up dates via email and call us when it feels right. There are so many of us, we could become a real drag on your time and mental health.

Did Pete put you down as Health Proxy (in place of me)? I asked him to. You are there, I am not. We can have both of us on, if that works. You can always reach me by phone and we can consult.

I want to know about the oxicodone. What is its function? What effect does it have on him? Will they bring it down as we proceed? He is uncomfortable but not experiencing pain as he tells it. I hope he is not cognitively undermined by the meds. That will make things worse I fear.

I await a word from you.............love, Sarah

Janeane did lay out everything and it had been a tough week for her. Pete's constipation had been so bad that he wept with frustration and bled from the rectum – very hard for a daughter to watch. And there had been an emergency trip to the hospital when he felt he couldn't breathe. She said she cried for three days after she got home. It was a relief to leave, to get back to three children and a demanding job -- but she also felt she shouldn't have left, and yearned to go back. This tension plagued Janeane and her relations with her aunt constantly. Janeane made the three-hour trip to Medford for the weekend several times, sometimes with her husband and children. It was a hard time.

At Pete's house, Elinor struggled with the borrowed laptop, trying hard to get on-line. Sarah left a frustrated phone message: "Where are you, we can't get through!"

Sarah, sorry ---I was on the Benkin help line for about an hour, trying to get the wireless system Willa provided to actually work. Fortunately it didn't – because then Pete got challenged, up and off the sofa, and became the hero! A moment of being his old self.

I think it will turn out that this job is easier for me than it was for Janeane. Being a daughter is much harder than bring a distant sister. She, Terrie and Alexis set things up very nicely for me. Terrie and Jim stayed while Janeane took the three hour round trip to pick me up in Concord and stayed for a little bit, but no one visited today, and it was OK. I was worried about too many visitors.

Pete is not befuddled by the meds (more detail when we talk) but he is very uncomfortable much of the time and is having much trouble eating. He has not changed the health proxy -- I'll talk with him about it more tomorrow. The DNR and Hospice status will cover most contingencies anyway.

Caro called at nine -- I assured her that once I get on line (as you can see, I am now), I will be able to send news to all concerned, without bothering her as an intermediary. She is doing a short message tonight. Pete and I have talked about when and whether I should buffer calls that come in to him -- that will change from time to time.

Lots more to learn still about the hospice people, doctors, terrain, shops......I am up for it!

Love............................Elinor

Dealing with the computer, with the gowing e-mail list of family and friends, with malfunctioning room monitors and call bells, was a constantly frustrating part of the next couple of weeks. Also, Elinor struggled to resist her own strong urge to tidy things up, because it seemed better to keep Pete's surroundings just as he preferred them, whether it went against the grain for her or not.

She tentatively asked if once or twice if Pete was worried about anything. He clearly did not want to hark back to his past, and he had no concept of heaven or hell that made him worry about the future.

At one point, she suddenly blurted out the story about having meningitis when she was twenty one, a young wife with a new baby and everything to live for. "I learned the function of pain

and misery," she told Pete. "It makes you willing to die."
"Yup," said Pete, and she realized that he was satisfied that she
understood the main thing she needed to know about his
condition.

Elinor wrote to the whole list again. It gave her and Pete both a
great sense of support to know that almost three dozen people
were thinking of him every day.

Pete's Progress, January 17, 2008:

*Hi, guys, Caro is encouraging me to write every day, even
when there is no "news."*

*In some ways, Pete is doing well. He gets up and half dressed
every day, checks the news on computer and TV, does some e-
mail, watches a history channel, reminisces with me about the
good old days, briefly greets his children, who do errands for
us and pass through occasionally. We watched Out of Africa
the other night, and a little bit of reading aloud has been fun.
I got a library card and will go back to the library for more
today or tomorrow.*

*The hard part is eating and drinking. Very hard to find things
Pete is willing to ingest. It has has to be very soft and, alas, it
often causes pain, nausea or hiccoughs almost immediately.
The topic of food is a constant even though it gets to be boring
and frustrating. Pete's inability to drink raises much concern
about hydration.*

*Pete has not complained of inability to breathe since I came
on January 12, and the draining of the pleural cavity at the
hospital in Concord last Tuesday went easily. He and Alexis*

did a wash of the abdominal cavity yesterday, the first since I came, and it went smoothly.

Having Alexis (22) and Lucelia(2) around is really wonderful. They are in and out of Pete's side of the house without ever getting in the way, and their voices and sounds in the background prevent the place from feeling like just a sick room.

Thanks to Willa, we have call bells and portable phones and room monitors all over the place, and have slowly learned how to put them to good use. Thanks to Terrie and Alexis, the house is clean and I have a good room to call my own. Thanks to Janeane, there is lots of food in stock.

Hospice is responsive, available 24/7. In response to Pete's request, they keep changing the meds for pain and nausea, hoping to find some combination which is really effective. So far, this has not been successful. I have been made "health proxy" for decisions if ever Pete cannot make them, instead of Sarah, as requested by her and Hospice. A DNR (do not resuscitate order) is in place.

Karen [Pete's youngest daughter] will come tomorrow for the long weekend. I will talk later today with Pete about visitors and let you know his thoughts on the subject.

I remember from my parents' waning days how hard it is to wait for news from afar, and I will try now to be better about writing daily. Caro will help. Feel free to call if you want to.

The first three days I was here, a lovely quiet snow fell almost constantly, but warm enough so that it has not made driving bad. I love seeing it.

More soon. Love to you all.

Cheers..Elinor

A book about dying arrived from Caro. Elinor showed it to Pete, offering to let him have a look first. "I don't want to look at it and I don't want to hear anything about it," he told her sternly. OK. She perused it herself, finding helpful stories and quotes from many writers on death and loss.

It seems that Pete refused any "deep discussions" with any sibling and child. He never spoke with Elinor about any fears or feelings. There was no review of his life or talk about his after-death future, though she made opportunities available. Once, months before she came to his house, on the phone, he had said about his coming death, "It doesn't matter." Now he continued to be in a detached, almost Buddhist state of mind, letting his concerns go one by one.

It was only the fine details of household operation and his own physical health that still disturbed him. *"What is the thermostat set at?" "Look at this little poop, no bigger than a marshmallow, and the same color!"*

Pete had lost his parents, a wife, two children and a grandchild, so he had had plenty of opportunity to observe and ponder the transition from life to death. It seemed clear that he expected

71

nothingness after death, and accepted the idea that his ego and awareness would disappear. Some family members had earlier tried to persuade him of a different scenario, but during these last weeks, they let him be, praying for him in their different ways.

Elinor thought perhaps physical touch would be a way to reach him and to relieve his pain. He allowed brief hugs, and the dressing changes from Alexis. Sometimes she could provide a bit of massage on hips or shoulders in the middle of the night. But you couldn't touch his hands or feet, still tingling and sensitive from neuropathy, and he couldn't lie on his bloated stomach for a back massage.

One night, to be companionable, he and Elinor sang little rounds from childhood, in croaking old voices: "White coral bells upon a slender stalk."

"Good thing no one can hear us," they agreed, but later it turned out that Chip and Alexis had been listening from their bedroom right above Pete's.

Pete's Progress, January 18

Hi, guys, we seem to have got the new meds regulated a bit better, though it is hard to tell for sure, and Pete is taking an anti-nausea pill in the wee hours -- it helps to prevent that early morning retching. Today has been going pretty well, fortunately, since a lot of visitors have come and gone.

Karen came! She left DC in the dark wee hours, got here at 10 am. Got in a good couple of hours with Pete before others started coming through. I got to go out, to Top's Plaza in Marsdale, for some grocery shopping. We all keep scouting for things Pete might be able to eat -- and keep down. The sun and shadow on the snowy rolling hills was gorgeous.

Willa came and hooked up the lap top to Pete's printer, also showed us how to use the cordless phones as an intercom. She did this despite chaotic goings-on in her own household this week. Terrie and Jim came by again. Karen's Aunt Karen may show up on Sunday for overnight, Monday being a holiday.

We have also heard that Caro and her husband are thinking of coming the last weekend in January, and that Curt [nephew] will drive Sarah[his mother] over February 2. Pete is OK so far with the idea of house-guests; he will just go off to his room if he gets weary, nauseous, or plagued by abdominal cramps, all of which happen a lot.

Gotta sign off for now -- I am keeping out of the way of Pete's visiting kids, using the lap top, and my battery is running low. More tomorrow.

Cheers......................Elinor

Keeping out of the way when Pete's children and friends came to visit was deliberate on Elinor's part, but it had a negative repercussion. "Shucks," she said, "they may have felt that I did not want to be friendly with them." Comfortable relations could not develop easily during such a stressful time, except among

73

those actually living in Pete's house. While some family members probably felt that Elinor had "taken over," she herself often felt invisible and ignored. These discomforts couldn't be helped just then.

Pete's Progress, January 19

Hi, guys, it is about six in the evening on Saturday. Karen has been here most of the days, talking in turns to me and to Pete.

Making the meds work for Pete as desired continues to be a challenge. Eating causes vomiting or abdominal cramps almost every time. Chills and hot flashes, dry mouth, muscle twitches, spells of faintness are part of the day. At least the hiccoughs have been substantially controlled.

Pete talked to a neighbor for a few minutes, and gave some instructions about money issues. Karen has gone to her in-laws for supper, but may come back for a while this evening. She is collecting Pete's stories and memories – she remembers her grandfather saying that this is where the real history of a people lies, in their family stories. (I am writing the same kind of stuff when I get free moments now and then, partly for her.)

The pace is very slow, but I am adapting pretty well, given my temperament. I've got a residual cough from a cold three weeks ago that is bothering me at night; I'll try a new regimen tonight.

But in many ways, this week has been much easier than my last week at home. Leaving my California life made me very empathetic to Pete leaving his earthly life. A person worries about how things will go without him, and mourns the people and other delights he is having to leave behind.

Also, I remember how hard it was for me to be 3000 miles away when my parent) were dying, so I know how your hearts are yearning towards Pete.

Not knowing what to expect in terms of duration and experience along the way is very frustrating for everyone, I know. Pete is "not eating enough to keep a bird alive," but his heart is strong and his vital signs are good despite his suffering. So it'll be a while yet, I would predict.

Send greetings and news -- we can put it all to good use.

Cheers.........................Elinor

Caro sent a note ending with

Yes, we hold you and especially Pete in our hearts. I talk about him with everyone all the time. Thanks for hanging in there with him. Caro

It felt good to complain a little bit to her in an e-mail.

Managing the machines and the e-mail list is hard for me, I am such a Neanderthal about these things. Harder in some ways is the slow pace. You know, my engines rev at sixty miles an hour, as you might say, and I feel as though I am holding the brakes on all the time. I knew I was signing on for simple housework and for "holding the basin," but I forgot how boring it could be. Boring but still busy. Pete gets gruff if I am not at his side in a minute after he calls. I will have walked many miles back and forth between rooms before this is over. I almost never get out or see anyone during the week. Fortunately, I've got library books, even one or two I couldn't get in San Francisco because the demand there was so great.

The room monitor and intercom systems could not be made to work adequately, so Elinor started sleeping downstairs near to Pete, on the sofa in the living room. It was quite comfortable, and the grandfather clock from their childhood was sort of reassuring. However, it took several nights before she stopped waking up every time it struck the hour. She was half awake anyway, listening for Pete. It was really bad when it rained: the rain drops on the skylight sounded just like Pete's footsteps creaking on the dining room floor.

Pete's Progress, January 20.

Hi, everybody,

Today's been Sunday, all day. Visitors came -- Karen, her Aunt Karen, Willa and her kids. Pete is mostly too weary to converse, so they all watched a long Transformer movie with him -- a pleasant afternoon. Alexis made a stew to share, and Pete ate two bites and half a strawberry. I drove to Marsdale for new meds and wrote a bit in my family stories series....

Had a long telephone chat with Sarah, but only because she was too woozy to leave her bed. Hmmm.

Usually these messages are written by me, checked for accuracy by Pete, and then forwarded by him to his Updates list, which I don't have on my PC.

But if, like tonight, he isn't up to checking, I am trying to get it sent on to my own list before nine pm. ... You may get it again tomorrow from Pete.

Send us news of you.

Cheers..Ellilee

Sarah is Pete's twin, and her serious intermittent dizziness and vertigo was mystifying everyone. Was it a sympathetic ailment? Was she totally "dizzied" by her twin brother's immanent death?

Shortly after this, Elinor laboriously transferred Pete's whole family-friends e-mail list one by one to her own borrowed laptop. Pete was no longer able to check or even read the reports. If people had sent their own news, probably he couldn't have taken it in.

Pete's progress, January 23

Well, the night and then the day was going along pretty well when suddenly, around 5:30 pm, despite plenty of meds to prevent it, Pete had a violent attack of vomiting again. Dismaying and exhausting for him, and hospice is perplexed, promising to consult MDs on Thursday.

So our day pretty much fizzled out, and we are all off to bed early.

As the song says so hopefully, "Tomorrow's gonna be another day--ay--ay--ay!"

Cheers.............................Elinor

At least Sarah was feeling better:

Oh dear darlings, I am so sorry to hear about the vomiting again. How I do sympathize with you. Such a joy to feel like myself again for the first time in over a week or even more. The pressure band you sent appears to be a blessing. I will go to the workshop in Vermont. Lots of love to you both. I hear that you will again have many guests this weekend. I will call tomorrow night. Sleep well and thanks again. Love you both.

Holly wrote asking about Pete's bank accounts. It's true that various transfers and clarifications were needed to get things set up the way Pete wanted for his kids. His son, Gordon, organized the materials, and then Elinor took Pete to banks on the way to and from doctor and hospital visits, separate trips being too hard on him.

There was one terrifying incident on the way to a bank. Elinor was driving on a two lane road, maybe forty miles an hour, in the snow, with a truck immediately behind them. Pete muttered something inaudible about pulling over, then immediately opened the car door and vomited out the side.

As Elinor calculated how fast to stop, she could see the truck right on her tail, and she could also see that Pete had nothing substantial to hang on to, no hand grip or dashboard ledge or anything. It is a miracle he didn't pitch right out on his head.

The vomiting was always like that, without any warning. After that, they equipped the car with an airplane sick-bag and a basin. Truth to tell, though, Pete never went out in the car again, except for one trip home from the hospital the next week. They stopped for the last bank transaction on the way that time. Pete went into the bank in pajamas.

===

Meanwhile, another sub-plot was played out. Pete had one son, Stan, who had become estranged many years earlier. In addition to conflict between father and son, some family theorists thought that his adoption into the family might have been a factor in his decision to cut himself off from the family later. It is thought that some adopted children, fearing a repeat of the original "abandonment" in their lives, do the abandoning themselves. *"If I leave you all now, you will never be able to leave me."* Pete and his other children had pretty much given up totally on Stan the year before, when Sonny died. Even when his brother died, Stan failed to appear or contact them.

But his aunt, Pete's sister Holly, made a hard decision. She wrote to Elinor on January 24:

> *I awoke yesterday morning wrestling with my conscience about Stan. I finally decided that if Stan doesn't want to know what's going on with his Pop, then he doesn't have to read about it. But I don't feel right depriving him of the information with or by which he could make an informed choice about whether or not to come to closure with Pete*

before his death. So -- I spent most of the day putting together an 18-page compilation of various people's contributions to "Pete's Progress Report" starting with the letter I wrote in December and continuing up to the present. I have to edit it down a bit before I deliver it to Stan. I will try and email it to him, but if it bounces back, I will hand-deliver it to his house. (He lives upstairs from his in-laws in a two-family house fairly close to me.)

Sarah said I should tell you that last paragraph. I'm not sure that you should mention it to Pete, though, in case my delivery has no effect.

Meantime, give my love to Pete.

Love,
Holly

No one told Pete, but other members of the family over the next weeks were glad to know that Stan had been informed. Later, too, Holly told Stan when Pete died, and informed him about the funeral. But he did not attend.

==

Pete dozed and napped a lot during the day time, but Elinor was up and about all day, and getting pretty sleep-deprived from waking so often during the night. So surely he wouldn't wake her for no good reason, right? Yet there he was at the side of the sofa, at 4 am, sounding grumpy and gruff.

 "Elinor, get up." She started up in alarm, "Oh. Pete, what's the matter?"

"Get up."

 "What? Are you OK?"

 "Yes. Get up."

"Why would he want me to get up again, if he was OK? God, I was so tired!" she said later.

"But I got up, and he led me to another room, to a window looking out onto his snowy back lawn. The sky was clear, the moon was full and brilliant. "There it is," he said, "the moon on the breast of the new fallen snow."

"And he was right to wake me for that. It was absolutely spectacular. It was his last gift to me. A treasure to remember."

Pete's Progress, January 25

A better day today, after a bad start. Pete's gone to using a patch for preventing nausea. Janeane and family will be here tomorrow and Sunday, so probably I'll get in a little shopping, and maybe, finally, church in Concord on Sunday.

Caro et al will be able to come later in Feb. after all.

Be well, guys.

Cheers........................Elinor

The real story was more grim than she was reporting. Five or six times a day, she would prepare pretty trays with little plates holding an array of carefully chosen food, and Pete would be able to eat only one strawberry, say, or one bite of custard. Alexis found a small silver tray and a set of little cups which were just right for his meals. She offered goodies from her own kitchen. The other family members brought delectables, and visitors plied them with food. But mostly Pete could not eat. He would reject what had seemed attractive the day before. The family lived off the leftovers, and also threw away inordinate amounts of spoiling food.

When Pete could eat, he would often vomit soon afterwards. He was prescribed pills to prevent this, but often would refuse to take them, or would vomit them up. Keeping to the hospice-prescribed regimen of meds was virtually impossible, so it wasn't clear if the medications were effective or not. The family became frustrated with the hospice staff and vice versa, although everyone was restrained and polite.

Elinor walked to the library once a week or so for books and movies to distract Pete (not too successful) and comfort herself (worked well). The library was a great boon to the town – you could see that the librarian served also as a lonely-hearts comforter for local folks. But the little village was dreadfully depressed economically, with no one walking about and most of the shops closed or struggling.

No matter, for mostly they were focused on the scene at home anyway. Elinor was bucked up almost daily by a cheery phone call from her eldest son in California.

==

Pete's Progress, January 27

Well, guys, we have had an adventuresome 24 hours. I didn't write last night at 8:30 as has become my custom because the ambulance summoned by Hospice arrived just about then, and I followed it on icy small roads in falling snow to the hospital twenty miles away. All because Pete had suddenly vomited black blood.

[Elinor had refrained from saying: "large amounts of black blood and clots and yuck." She kept the whole bucket for the hospice nurse to see when he arrived at high speed and called the ambulance.]

Twenty four hours later, after stomach drain, CAT scan, and new medications, the current status is:

--Pete is much more comfortable tonight, his second in hospital, than he has been for a week.
--His GI tract is not blocked by a new eruption of cancer. Possibly he has an ulcer from all the meds. He is on a new drug for gastric acid.
--He will probably come home tomorrow, with medicinal patches for nausea and pain, currently being controlled by IV drugs.
--The squeezed lung has collapsed, which may mean there is no longer need for pleural cavity draining every week. The other lung is functioning OK and Pete is no longer suffering from shortness of breath, esp. given that he is moving around only very little.
--There is virtually nothing draining from the old port in the right side of his abdomen, but there is a pocket of fluid on

83

*the other side now. Tomorrow morning, Pete and the MD
will decide whether to drain that off by CAT-scan-guided
needle before he leaves the hospital.
--No fever, vital signs good, ambulance volunteer who
forgot his bag here has retrieved it, and the neighbors
alarmed by the ambulance have been reassured.
--I got to and from Concord in the wee hours, via barely
known route and car, on narrow icy roads sprinkled with
new snow, without mishap. Whew. Went and returned in
half the time in daylight today.
--Janeane, here as cook and companion for Pop during the
day Saturday, joined me at the hospital for several hours
today as well.
--Gordie hosted Janeane and her whole family of five,
including meals, throughout the weekend, tho' preparing for
surgery on his own leg tomorrow. Blessings on him.
--Alexis passed news back and fore by phone, washed
everything from Pop's bed while he was away, cleaned the
oven, and kept the homefires burning.
--People from all over called or sent e-messages.*

It takes a village.

Love.......................Ellilee

She sent another message later in the day:

*Hi, guys, one of my California friends looked up Pete on the
Internet and was impressed. Read here:*

> *I'm sorry to hear of Pete's trip to the hospital. I was thinking
> about calling you yesterday, so I googled Pete Bowers of
> Medford, NH, and up came not only an address and phone*

number, but Barkley bus driver; Concord Peace Vigil; union activities; a letter to Scientific American; and Barkley's Center for Religion, Ethics, and Social Policy. An interesting brother you have!

Pete's Progress, January 28, via Caro in New York City:

Elinor got home from the hospital today to find that she couldn't get her own PC up and running, so she asked me to send a few lines about their day. Please note that I'm sending these to my list only, so if you know other people that should be on the list, feel free to forward.

Pete was better today than he has been for weeks. His first day in hospital he was on an IV [intravenous tube]. But that has been removed and, with the other interventions completed, he has been able to drink lots today: jello, tea, water and chocolate soy milk. A veritable feast! Furthermore, he and Elinor "went out to eat," all the way down to the hospital cafeteria, with Pete walking there, jauntily, no doubt.

Although Pete maybe could have gone home today, he himself asked for an extension til tomorrow morning, just to be sure he is fully stabilized. He will go home, then, with two patches: one for nausea and one for pain. These should eliminate the thorny problem of taking pills on a queasy stomach. Th patches stay on for about three days each and can be replaced at home. Hospice will still be coming daily.

Since Saturday, Elinor has been going home at night, but spending the entire day at the hospital. She has learned the

85

road to the hospital backwards and forwards through ice and snow and is looking forward to bringing Pete home tomorrow in dry conditions.

Last I heard, Sarah was in Boston, waiting for Holly, who would take her home! Apparently she is fine, too, and will, undoubtedly, add her news under separate cover.

Cheers to all………………… Caro

Pete's Progress

Chapter 4: Things Get Tough

Pete's Progress, January 29

Well, folks, the plot has thickened. I went to the Med Center early this a.m. with the intention of bringing Pete home with me (via the bank, as there is still unfinished business there). He was in fine fettle last night, walking around the ward with me, checking his e-mail, ready to go home in the morning.

But one look at him today and I saw that he was totally snowed, grogged out. Feeling no pain or nausea, but deeply asleep, twitchy, hallucinating slightly, muttering strange incantations, offering half sentences with big words and no coherence. If you really got in his face, he could wake up and respond, even recognize people. A few times he sipped liquid, took a pill. Once he tottered to the john with a nurse and squeezed out a few drops. But mostly he couldn't stay awake all day, muttered weird words, and grasped at invisible objects.

It took hours for doctors and hospice people to show up. Everyone agreed: maybe his starved, dehydrated body, his drug-injured gut and partially functioning kidneys, were hypersensitive to the many meds he had been given PRN ("as needed") in the last 24 hours. Or maybe the big C is just finally winning the battle.

So they discontinued a lot of the drugs, and we all agreed to wait until Wednesday morning to see what will happen. If he is not better tomorrow a.m., it will indicate that he is on the downward path. It is not expected to be fast -- many days and maybe longer. His vital signs are good, his heart is strong, his one good lung is functioning well, he has bowel and bladder control, he can stand up and walk a bit.

I had a chance to review all this with Sarah and Holly this evening by phone -- they are together at Sarah's tonight.

Alexis came with a supportive friend to visit at the hospital. They both wept. Alexis changed Pete's abdominal dressing—she is better at it than the hospital staff. But no more draining of gut or pleural cavity is planned. She and her husband and a friend are going to replace the leaking sink in Pete's bathroom tonight. It's a funny time, but they just <u>have</u> to do something for him. Everyone is trying to help. Willa fixed the answering machine. Janeane is coming back again tonight, partly to support her siblings. Gordon had surgery yesterday for a clot in his leg, and everyone has complications in their lives. No tears are falling but you can feel how we are all afloat.

We have had a bevy of good wishes by e-mail and welcome them all. It really makes a difference to know that people are aware of what's going on here.

Cheers.........................Elinor

Sarah wrote to everyone:

Dear Everyone,

I just talked to Elinor and I ask that we all hold our Pete gently and lovingly over the next hours. The next twenty four hours will be crucial to his journey. Hours, days or even weeks, this feels like the last leg of the journey.

Pete has stood by many who have died, and I trust that we all will hold him in our hearts as he finds his way out of our time and place here and now.

Love, Sarah

While Pete was in the hospital for three days, at least Alexis and Elinor got to sleep well at night. But sitting with him at the hospital doing nothing just about drove Elinor berserk. At one point the hospice social worker helped by telling her to go out and drive around the town a bit.

A message came from niece Banny, one of Holly's daughters.

I don't know what to say that won't come out as cheesy or contrived, but I did just want to tell Pete that I love him and that I know there are so many others in his life who love him dearly as well and that is the mark of a truly great life. I am praying for his comfort all the time and for comforting all of those who are with him and thinking about him with great heaviness of heart. Pete had a bunch of hard knocks in life but he endured in a most heroic manner, in a way I'm not sure I could have in similar circumstances. I admire him for that. I can only imagine how tired he must be at this juncture and yet he goes on fighting. From what I hear, he doesn't really complain much, just takes it in stride. Again -- admirable.

I like thinking of Pete at our first family reunion, goading everyone to sing as we sat on the stumps in a circle one night. One song in particular, Down by the Bay, which has always been a favorite of mine, brings a particular smile to my face. I can't say that I have nearly as many memories of Pete as others in the family, but I do have many fond ones all the same. In my mind Pete had many quirks, but really, who doesn't, especially in this crazy family of ours. We are truly a motley crew if ever one existed!

Keep your chins up, everyone, and just keep loving each other as you do. Remember that a merry heart doeth good like a medicine. Make jokes, even if someone may accuse you of being callous. Laughter does wonders!

Love, Banny

Banny's letter was one of several they got which were like funeral tributes coming in advance. They were all suffering from "anticipatory grief," as the books call it.

Sometimes grief turns into anger. At one point, Elinor got into a rage which she did not share with the family. She sent her January 29 report to her women's group in Arizona, which includes three nurses, complaining about the hospital staff and how they overdosed Pete so badly. Actually, both hospice and hospital staff were involved in the decisions, and you couldn't pin responsibility on anyone.

Well, girls, see especially paragraph three below.

I didn't say the following to my family (except sister Sarah by phone), but I am furious. Was it gross incompetence or were they deliberately trying to take him out? Hot damn! For all I know, this is how they do it these days, pretending that he needed more meds. Moreover, for all I know, he could have secretly asked for them to do it.

Either way, they messed up. If they were aiming for symptom control, they should have known better than to give him 40 mg of Oxycodone when he was already established (24 hours) on a Fentanyl patch (as well as a scopolomine patch), and then add Ativan for anxiety and Thorazine for hiccups (which were never serious or prolonged) and possibly other meds as well, all within an eight hour span, on a radically empty and drug-injured stomach, with a malfunctioning kidney.

On the other hand, if they were aiming to off him, they should have known it would take more than that for a young guy with such strong vitals.

But still, we are not complaining. Why? Because he was not uncomfortable today, just semi-comatose and crazy. Because people are inexorably human. And because he is going to die anyway. Shit.

I have had a day full. To bed.

Cheers...........................Elinor

Nurse Kathy responded immediately, bless her heart.

Oh Elinor, what you describe sounds so gut wrenching especially for you, watching all this & wanting relief for your brother.......and yet, it may be less difficult for him because in the process of what happened he may actually have been pain free for a while &/or may have little memory of the experienc. What you describe sounds so typical to me.........let me explain my thinking & I suspect that Dierdre & Anna may provide other perspectives.

I wasn't aware that your brother had gone in the hospital, so am not sure the reason, but I do know that in one of your recent e-mails you did report that "it is nigh well impossible to control Pete's pain and nausea". My guess is that during the night, he became quite uncomfortable & that because ALL these meds were already ordered on his chart on a prn basis, they were given despite the interactions because the staff also had difficulty seeing him in such distress & he may have been asking for something, anything to relieve his discomfort (not necessarily to bring things to an end).

I also know that unless there is a real hotshot MD or NP/RN who is a pain control specialist, that often getting symptom control is hit & miss & unpleasant side effects result till the correct med(s) & dosages are worked out.

As for the meds ordered, I have known of people who became overly sedated from Fentanyl alone; it has at least a 17 hour half life, so once the patch is removed, it still remains in the system.

I have heard of people "getting confused" from wearing a scopolamine patch just for motion sickness.......

Thorazine (low dose, I think) was at one time the drug of choice used for hiccups; there are probably other/better choices available now.

Yes, absolutely, all these drugs interact & cause side effects, especially in a debilitated patient. I have seen this happen. It's not pleasant for anyone - especially family & staff, believe it or not. It's not unusual to have numerous meds prescribed for a variety of symptoms. Adding drugs, even with Fentanyl, is common practice.

Elinor, I don't think anyone was "trying to take out your brother". Incompetence? Hard to judge from here. Perhaps it was just that your brother was finally in a place where others saw how incredibly uncomfortable he is and tried to address it.......doing it all in one night probably wasn't the best answer....... the result may be that his medical team is now much more aware of his distress & perhaps a more effective pain/symptom control plan can be established.

Blessings on Pete, you & all your family as this time of saying good-bye to him draws nearer.

I do not take lightly your anguish as you witness his process & try to intervene for him. (Hopefully the Hospice staff will now step up to the plate.) I am simply sharing thoughts based on my own experiences, outdated as they may be.

Maybe some of the others of our group have more enlightened perspectives.

Elinor, hugs to you & please stay in touch.

Love, Kathy

Elinor was so grateful.

Kathy, you are a darling to take so much effort with your response.

I just brought Pete home, weaned from half of these meds, with the PRN dosages cut in half -- and that is where I think they went wrong, in ordering amounts excessive for someone with an empty gut and marginally functioning liver and kidneys. And there was one outright error. The thing is, they had a palliative care specialist, so they might have been expected to anticipate over-sensitivity to all the meds they piled on.

They pushed us gently to agree to a discharge today, and I see how the finances affect things. Hospice gets $250 or something per day -- they have to pay the hospital bill out of that, which must be $1000 a day or so. Anyway, I think it is right to have Pete home again, and of course, the professionals cannot stop the inexorable progression of the disease. So I am OK with it, though slightly nervous about the role I must play.

Anyway, now Pete is sleepy, slightly delirious from time to time, but able to walk, talk, eat and drink tiny amounts, move bowel and bladder tiny amounts. He is basically pain free. But nausea is again an issue because they took off the scopolamine patch 24 hours ago. We are back to compazine suppositories and crossed fingers on that. He's got me as his nurse, and his kids to do the drug store runs.

Stand by for more info from time to time.

Cheers..................Elinor

Another friend from the group, a hospice nurse herself, sent a classic letter which could go to any hospice family anywhere.

Elinor,

My heart goes out to you and all you are going through. Pete is so lucky to have you there for him. It is right for you to question and try to understand all that is happening. It is right to expect a quick response from hospice, most especially when he is home.

Managing pain and numerous other symptoms is such a difficult balancing act, especially in cancer. Patients and their families hope to be as physically and mentally alert and functional as possible, while keeping pain in control. This is very challenging. But there are many options and adjustments that can be made and it sounds like experts are there for you. (There are so many medical centers that don't even have palliative care specialists.) The need to adjust medication doses and even change medications can occur often toward the end of life. So do keep in touch with the hospice staff (I believe they are on call for you 24 hours a day?) ...

Elinor, you have all it takes to be the best nurse for Pete. Astute observational skills, a need to question, understand and advocate, devotion and most of all Love. I'm holding you in my heart.

Love, Dierdre

Later, discussing the episode further with these friends, Elinor understood better that hospice nurses working with cancer patients, especially independent-minded ones like Pete, always have to proceed by trial and error. Hospice nurses always know that the medications they propose may not be effective with that particular patient. In this case, the hospice nurse failed to make that completely clear. Each time he proposed a change in meds, the nurse would talk as though he was sure this would be the perfect answer. It never was. Often his own supervisors would countermand his idea. Often their joint proposals wouldn't work, either.

==

Pete's Progress, January 30.

Hi, guys, today there is a zig in this zig- zag course of ours. I really liked the male nurse who came on duty at the hospital at 7 last night and was eager to hear my concerns. So I called this morning before he was due to leave at 7 am.

He said Pete had a good night, steadily improved. They offered him liquids every two hours or so, walked him around the unit, got him to pee a bit. Seems like he is coming out of his drug haze.

I am setting off for the hospital now and will report again this evening. Meanwhile, I had a good sleep last night. And Pete's bathroom is half way through an overhaul which went long into the night and involved half his kids in one way or another. :)

Cheers..........................Elinor

==

Pete's Progress, January 30

Dear Ones,

Pete's progress today has included coming clear of the drug overdose, coming home from the hospital, and finishing some personal business items. He had a lovely deep-sleep nap in his own bed once home this afternoon. But he is not the man he was. Eating is still nearly impossible for him.

Janeane is here again, for a day or two, which is lovely. Sarah and Curt still plan to come Friday, though Sarah's own status is poor -- Holly has been with her for 2-3 days. We'll see how the twin sibs do together this weekend.

Alexis and her family work mates did a great job renovating Pete's bathroom while he was in hospital. They finished about 15 minutes before I brought him home today. Tiny Lucelia "helped" by staying with her grandma (aka Terrie) for a day and a night, but she was here to come around with hugs and wish us all "night-night" again today.

"The land was sweet and good. We did what we could."

Cheers..............................Elinor

==

Often at home, Pete had refused to take the meds as prescribed. But at the hospital, he liked the non-nonsense administration of meds on the hour as prescribed, and back at home, he became more cooperative, even when he had to be woken up to take pills or suppositories. At the hospital, food was served three times a day instead of six, so now at home, too, they dropped back to three.

One evening, Pete gave a serious little speech about not wanting to eat any more. It seemed like a milestone, but to make sure, they offered food again the next day, and he still ate a bite or two at meal times. Their efforts waned, though, as clearly keeping him minimally nourished was just prolonging his misery.

Meanwhile, it was very worrisome that Sarah, Pete's twin, living only three hours away, was still so sick, suffering from dreadful bouts of vertigo, off sick from work, almost unable to fulfill her usual role as the center stone of the whole extended family. Sarah is sort of psychic, so the family was wondering if, as his twin, she was at some level trying to take Pete's illness from him.

==

On January 30, a great testimonial came from Pete's adopted black son, Gordie.

Well to anyone who cares or might want to know ,i had surgery to remove a average size blood clot in my left lower leg.. ... So i'm taking my first drugs, and i hate it,cause i am so against that stuff. I shall be off for the week or more,yea super bowl coming up. But hopefully i will be mobile

98

enough to go visit my father who needs me and needs us more than i need anyone. He is my hero,and if i can be half the person he has been in any situation close to his down the road,i will be grateful to him. Watching him has really impressed me and actually has motivated me into wanting to do things people will see in the future. Its kinda weird, but i am knowing that he is going after this 110% and thru my years of coaching ball to kids and playing sports, i am very competitive as we all know. But to see my dad really never in that type of action, but to see him now, and he is going as hard as i would have running a touchdown for medford back in the day, is so awesome and just makes me look at life in a different way. I could never and would never want a different father ever. Anything good i have ever done is because of him, and he has taught me so well. I may not be Bowers blood thru and thru, but i know and feel like i am truly 100% his son. My saying to everyone is never give up don't ever give up. Anyhow leg is killing me, i'm going to bed.

===

A close family friend wrote:

Good Grief! as some of your family used to say. Elinor, it is purely wonderful that you are there doing what you are doing. I've been in like situations, so I have some idea of what it's like, but obviously not mostly.

Your progress notes are terrific, and it means a lot to me to get them and keep up day-to-day. Sounds like the family is rallying around in all sorts of configurations, which is lovely and heartwarming. Obviously Pete is a trooper. I

99

had a really good visit (from my perspective) with him, as well as Holly and Hunter and Millie, when he and Holly came down for the December time at CTCA in Philly. I told him then that I'm very flexible and can be called on for almost anything ....

Another personal friend in California wrote to Elinor, ending with this lovely phrase: *"I hold my hand out to you several times a day."*

Pete's Progress, January 31

It was another better day hereabouts today.

Despite the daily bout of vomiting and various aches and pains, Pete was up more this afternoon, ate a bit, and did some planning with his kids in person and by phone. Hospice nurses came. Their plan for Pete did not match the hospital discharge plan, so we talked until we got that sorted out.

I got my own paperwork and some of Pete's organized.

We are ready for snow tomorrow and Sarah and Curt(her son) Saturday. Sarah has got a new, treatable diagnosis-- something about Lyme Disease and an inner ear infection. She has started on a thirty day regimen of antibiotics.

Cheers.........................Elinor

It was a better day, but it ended in confusion when a planned family supper fizzled out with no explanation by the planners. Communication seemed to break down completely. Elinor remarks, "Maybe everyone wondered what he or she had done wrong; I certainly did. No one seemed to dare to say a word"

Then Gordie wrote to everyone again, giving voice to the confusion and anxiety many of Pete's children were feeling about what would happen to the family home and other assets. Many people responded to his message with concern and reassurance.

> *To those that lie and think that i don't know what is going on. Enjoy the house, money, furniture, etc. Certain people should not have been involved ,and that means grand kids, cousins etc. My main concern was about being fair, honest, and the welfare of my father. But i guess fair and honest are not spoken in this family except by a certain few. Pop i love you, thanks for everything. But i will not be at the funeral as of now and i am pulling out of everything. Bye.*

Pete's kids had been raised in that house, and Gordie had lived there for years as an adult. So had Terrie and Alexis. Also, they had been raised on the edge of poverty, but now, they knew, there was substantial money from the court settlement. But Pop wasn't making the decisions any more. What the heck was happening?!

Gordie wrote to Elinor personally:
> *Since you are in charge of everything, what i wanna know is, was the house given to Alexis. I don't want any excuses no bologna the truth is what i want. And if so i firmly believe they should be buying it from the immediate six ,as*

101

pop originally planned. I myself though was told this anonymously, and am concerned. It makes no sense to me, since i was offered to try and buy it, but with no price given, but yet am told it is writen and they get it free and clear. I am very hurt by this, and just want the truth. Also talking with Janeane about 2008 gifts and loans that were forgiven i am not exactly sure if we all have recieved what we were supposed to.

Dealing with such distress was a new task for a caregiver who had just been fixing the food, doing the laundry and holding the basin! But it wasn't unexpected. Elinor knew people were going to take their dismay out on her. She wrote back.

Gordie, thanks very much for writing again and working on sorting this all out.

Here's the best I can tell you just now.

I am not involved in the distribution of Pete's money at all. I wish you and Janeane had come yesterday to talk to him about it.

I know he intends that after his death, his assets, including the value of the house and vehicles, should be shared equally among the six kids. But I do not know anything about what he has given, loaned, and forgiven to you all in the past, and I cannot get involved in that. You and Janeane can ask Pop about it any time.

Pete simply asked me to organize his papers and pay the bills that keep coming, of course, since the time you and Janeane each did some of them with him. I have done that

102

and everything appears to be in pretty good order. After Pete's death, all that will be handled by the executor, which I believe is to be Janeane. (She can get help, and funds to pay for help, as she thinks necessary.)

Pete also asked me to make sure that he actually has a current will -- which he does not at the moment, so the lawyer is helping him update it. The main thing will be to remove the reference to your old debt, which is now paid. I don't think he intends any other changes.

Pete is eager to know that the funeral etc has been arranged and the bills paid. Janeane was taking the lead in that, and we were expecting to hear from her yesterday or today about that.

Pete talked with the hospice social worker in my hearing at the hospital about the house. Pete was eager to figure out a way that you, Gordon, could afford to buy it now or later, and he came up with the idea of you sharing it with someone else so you could get some rental income out of it.

Later, when you and Janeane were talking at the table here, I heard you say such a plan was unlikely to work. But something else might -- it'll be for you all to figure out. Pete has said that his main concern is that the house be sold to a family member or someone else, so that the value can be divided equally among the six children.

I know what a hard time this is for both of you, and for the rest of the family. I am glad to help the best I can.

Cheers......................Elinor

She sent Janeane a copy of that letter, and Janeane responded promptly.

Elinor,

Thank you for taking the time to sort this out. Splitting everything among the six of us was our understanding as well. Gordie and I have been asking questions, because we knew of a few discrepancies and issues with the accounts and we are just trying to make sure that everything is accounted for as it should be and more importantly that it is consistent with what Pop wants. It seems like every week some new issue comes up. It makes us a little nervous wondering when the next unknown problem will surface. So Gordie and I have been asking questions in an attempt to make sure everything is set while Pop can still participate.

Regarding the funeral home, I have called them three times and asked that they call back to Gordie's house, but they haven't yet. So I will call again on Monday. Here again it is confusing to me that you and Pop made a call to them and a package or plan was agreed upon, but yet no one can tell me what that is and I have to call and find out myself. Why are things being handled that way? It feels like you and Pop start things and then pass them on just to pacify my desire to be involved.

Karen and I have arranged to take leaves from work and come and help. I think we should come up with a plan that will be agreeable for us to do that. I think I would stay at Gordie's and Karen would stay with her in-laws.

Also, Pop had a good idea about renting a room for family to come and stay in. I am thinking we could get a better rate if we looked for a long term rental. It might be cheaper than weekends.

Our family really appreciates everything that you are doing for our father. It's a tough job and you are stuck in the middle.

Thanks,   Janeane

Terrie apologized for upsetting Gordie and explained her point of view.

Dear Gordon & Family,

I'm so sorry for being angry, to be honest with you all, I'm scared, and I'm hurting. I know we all are. We're all grieving in our own ways. We all have been through a lot, especially when it comes to <u>death.</u> We have lost so many family members that we love, and I know <u>death.</u> It's an ugly word to me, I hate it and <u>scares me.</u> But what I really want to say is that I'm very sorry to all my siblings that I couldn't save our brother, and I'm realizing, at least I think I am realizing, that I can't save Pop. Believe me all, I really did do my best for Sonny and for Pop. I did everything I thought I could do to make Sonny better. I wanted Sonny home, with all of us, so he could be with family. But Sonny is gone and everyday I miss him, and I know we all do.

When Pop first told me that he had cancer, when I was living on the other side of Pop's house, I told him that we would beat it, I told him I would do anything I could to help. Please believe me all of you, I really thought I helped Pop and that the cancer was all gone. I did everything I could do to take care of our father, because I knew that I was not ready to lose another loved one. I see that I failed with Pop, its out of my hands now. So again everyone, I'm sorry. I love you all so very much, and I did not want to see us go through this again. I want us all to be strong for each other. I need you all more that you think. I don't feel strong, I feel weak and scared. So please, let's not shut each other out, let's try to let by gones be by gones, and go on together as one. I know that's what Pop would want.

I Love you all so very much,

Terrie

Oooof. These were anguishing messages to write and to read. Elinor was glad that throughout all this time, her own eldest son was still calling every day, full of energy and good humor and local news from California. What a blessing!

===

Pete's Progress, February 1

Hi, guys,

Not too much weather locally, while the rest of New Hampshire was blizzardy, I gather. Still, we didn't go out anywhere, naturally.

Because the vomiting continues (soon after eating, despite various Rx), Pete got the scopolamine patch restored this am.

It'll take a few more hours to kick in completely. He has been moving very slowly today. It is hard for him to concentrate on stuff.

The sinks backed up and we had to call a plumber.

It'll be good to have Sarah and Curt here tomorrow and Sunday.

Cheers.................Elinor

Pete came to Elinor's sofa in the middle of the night again. He gestured brusquely for her to move her feet back, and then he sat down, more or less on her feet. No talk. He laid his head back, and they both dozed on and off for about an hour. If that was all the comfort he was going to accept, it was OK with her. After a while, he got up, said "See you in the morning, "and shuffled off to his own bed.

Several times afterwards, as he was going to bed for the night, she invited him to "visit" in the night if he wanted, but he only once came and sat with her the same way again.

===

Pete's Progress, February 2

Curt is a good son and escort, and has brought Sarah to see her twin. Sarah is doing OK, thank goodness, though still to dizzy to drive. We sat down at table like a family for both lunch and dinner.

Pete has had less vomiting and acute pain, but he is groggy with the heavier meds, has to sleep a lot, and still suffers from aches and pains and, this evening, some shortness of breath.

Family members hereabouts are sorting out a variety of issues. It is a time of grief and anxiety. Phew. We are tired.

Sarah says you gently mock me for ending my notes with my habitual sign-off, "cheers." She offers alternatives: Cheers through the tears. Cheers through the fears. But fears and tears do not loom large for me and Pete, it seems. Fatigue, endurance, patience are issues. Frustration.

Well, shit! ....Elinor

(Is that better than "cheers"? It made Curt and Sarah laugh, anyway.)

Actually, in the context of mourning and misery and advanced sleep deprivation, this criticism hurt Elinor deeply. Weeks later, to her astonishment, some one raised it again, and she explained in more detail.

Though no Pollyanna, it is part of my intention in life to "walk cheerfully over the earth." Being consistently cheerful with and for Pete and his children was a major part of my task in Medford.

Being cheerful that particular weekend was hard. Elinor had anticipated that she would become "the lightening rod" for family distress, and she talked about it with the hospice social worker. But it is always hard to be wrongfully accused, to be considered guilty until proven innocent. Why could people not just ask questions instead of making accusations? Sister Sarah helped a lot by providing a listening ear by phone for people who were angry at Elinor. "I just did my house work and wrote my "Pete's Progress" reports," she says.

Pete's Progress, February 3

Pete came in and out from the bedroom to join us today, as we watched Michelle Obama and the Super Bowl etc. ("We" means Sarah, Curt, myself and then various Pete-family people coming and going.) But even on the sofa, Pete snoozed much of the time, cuz he is weary and drugged up. He ate two little squares of cantaloupe for breakfast and a green bean for lunch -- Curt noted that at least he has a good distribution of fruit and vegetables in his diet. Oy.

Sarah helped sort through logistics for "coverage" here in the coming weeks, talking with me and Janeane in turn. We'll be in touch with others soon.

Keeping cheerful on purpose,

Yours.............................Elinor

===

Gordie took over from Janeane the task of making funeral arrangements, and Sarah helped get information from Pete. Elinor sent an update to Gordie.

Gordie, after the mortician called you and you called here this morning, Sarah annoyed Pete with questions. But at least we were able to find out that he envisages 1) the more generous funeral plan with a rented casket and extra "calling hours" like you wanted; 2) cremation; and 3) burial of the ashes in the plot near Sonny. I understand that Janeane and Willa have been working on the details of the funeral and cemetery arrangements.

Pete has named Janeane as executor, and thought he had talked to her about that.

He has a life insurance policy which he believes is current. (By the way, that will not have to go through probate, I am pretty sure.)

Pete said you should ask him about these things directly. He is ready for all of us to handle everything we can.

Cheers.................................Elinor

Pete's children were surprised that he had requested cremation, and confused, because he had also spoken about the grave site. These new directions explained the strange mention of a "rented" casket. His body would be displayed in the casket; then after the viewing and the funeral, his body would be cremated. In the spring, after the ground thawed, his ashes would be buried at the grave site.

As these arrangements were completed, another testimonial admiring Pete came from Karen's aunt Karen, sister of Pete's second wife, Jeri. Unfortunately Pete no longer seemed to have any interest in such messages.

Hello!

The other night I sat at the keyboard composing a letter to send to everyone on your list. It basically was my thoughts, memories etc..., however in trying to send it, it was erased. Sorry. I just wanted you to know how much I admire Pete for his courage, his unending search for new and better treatments, and his calm and brave manner in the face of such adversity. I myself would be a basket case.

My memories of Pete are intertwined with the happiness he brought my twin sister, Jeri. Although their time together was short lived, it was full and enriched by the arrival of Karen Kay. Jeri's death left a big hole in my heart. Pete has always made me feel welcome and has allowed me to take Karen on visits and vacations with us (all which helped my slow healing), and I thank him for those precious moments. Pete, you did a wonderful job raising Karen and I know you must be as proud of her as I am. I have never heard you raise your voice and you always seem to take things in stride -- qualities I wish I possess.

That does one say at a time like this - words cannot express the sorrow that I feel. I often ask why bad things happen to good people and feel it isn't fair. I was thrilled that Pete could walk Karen Kay down the aisle and I love the picture of the Bowers clan at the reception. You can just see the joy and love in everyone's faces. I am thankful for having met and spent time with all of you. I wish I could be up there to support Pete and the family in any possible way. My thoughts and prayers are with all of you.

Much Love, Karen

Pete's twin, Sarah, went back home and wrote to everyone about her visit:

Dear Everyone:

I am just home from two days at Pete's. Curt drove me up. The energy there has shifted, and the quiet and relatively easy flow of Sunday comes with considerably more consistent and patch- dispensed meds, a pain med that Pete can control and Elinor sticking fast to the schedule agreed on by hospital, Hospice and Pete.

Pete has found his comfort level and security in the quiet gentle consistancy of Elinor. When I appeared when he called, I was dismissed (gently) and Elinor's word was required for reassurance.

He is like a man waiting for the train, his bags are packed his ticket bought, and he has left the world behind him and is bound for ...... The train is not yet here but he is anxious to be free to get on when it does. Being called to look back, worry about a last supper, an unpaid bill or a lost button is an unnecessary imposition. He stated clearly that he loved everyone, that there was nothing he had left undone that we all couldn't handle and that he is weary of the waiting.

As Elinor has described so clearly, he was with us only as he could be, as we celebrated the politics of the future, the touchdown that suddenly meant nothing and the inconceivable joys of an ice cream sundae.

Lucelia (age 2) looks at Pete and knows that things have shifted. She is quiet and super sensitive to where her pop-pop is.

I am ever so grateful to Alexis who is always there and Celie who promises tomorrow and Chip who comes home like clockwork, and is up and out early the next morning. Life goes on.

I am impressed with our commitment to work through the hurdles of misperceptions and projections from a dozen different perspectives, no one ever having the whole picture.

I am confident that the older generation will remember this time with its highs and its lows as we remember our parents' dying, and remember that miraculously in the end we were closer, not further apart.

And I am grateful to the universe and how this entire scenerio has been laid out. The pieces have fallen where they are needed and the roles have been cast by an extraordinary director. Gordie, Janeane, Willa, Terrie, Karen and Pete create a circle of love that so many of the rest of us lean into and feed. Elinor is there hour after hour, week after week. Her act of love for Pete and all the rest of us, is apparent. It is not easy, it is not without a dozen pitfalls but what I have seen is that we are learning to pick up the life of Pete Bowers, let it infuse us, know that he loves us and know that is why we love him.

Sigh...Father told me once that "a sigh was a call to the great Comforter."

Sarah

Her son, Curt, also wrote to the whole list.

I thought I would also try to share my perspective of this past weekend, however the nightly emails from Ellilee and my mom's email have painted a very clear and poignant picture already.

As my mom has so eloquently stated, Pete is clearly ready to move on to the next chapter, whatever that might be. For the most part he is very gentle and sweet and there are moments when he sounds like good old Pete, throwing out a sarcastic comment or two. He doesn't seem to be in much pain and his nausea wasn't that bad for the time we were there. He has all but stopped eating, but did join us at the table for at least one meal a day. He sleeps much of the day and when he is awake he is mostly quiet and still, but he is very responsive when asked a direct question. His memory is still very strong and he helped Ellilee and my mom remember stories from their childhood throughout the weekend.

While there are moments of clarity he is often seemingly out of it whether he is asleep or spacing out. It is evident that the drugs keep him fairly groggy but they also seem to be doing their part in keeping the pain and discomfort at bay.

Ellilee has been and continues to be an incredible support system for Pete, not to mention all of us who cannot be there for the day-to-day. She is very diligent that Pete takes his medicine on time and always has food ready for him, even

114

though for the most part he isn't very interested in it. She is very attentive and sensitive to his needs. It was also evident that between Alexis, Janeane, Celie, and the rest of his family, Pete is truly rich with support and love.

It seems to me that while it will not be easy for any of us, Pete feels that he has done what needs to be done and the rest will be left to us, including letting him go. As we move forward it will be very important that we remember to be there for each other and to be patient with one another. I realized as I pulled up Pete's driveway that I hadn't been there since I was little and that it is a shame that this is what is bringing me back. I know we are all busy with our lives but moving forward I would hope that we keep these lines of communication and family connection open.

I will always be grateful to Pete not only for his presence in my life as a wonderful uncle, or as an example of living your faith (whether it be religious or moral), but also as my mother's most constant and steadfast companion. He means so much to all of us in different ways and he will certainly be missed and always be remembered. May we be as graceful and courageous as he as we take this next step.

Love to you all,

Curt

==

In Medford, the strain was hard, but most people were keeping a stiff upper lip. Gordie had already lost a brother to estrangement and a brother to death; he was going to be the only remaining

115

male in the family. Again, he was the main one among them all who could express the pain. He had another huge spasm of grief and anger which he shared with the whole long e-list of family and friends. Because it seemed as though no one of Pete's children could afford to buy the family home where Pete had lived for 27 years, Gordie and his siblings were faced with losing the house as well as their father.

Am i a bad person? From what i'm hearing there seems to be alot of talk about me and my lifestyle. What i have done or not done. I'm the black guy. Am i a racist? I don't think so, but others do. People wanna talk about things that they think about me, and then lie to my face. Or think i don't hear anything and then look at me as if their innocent. Right now to tell you the truth the only brother i feel i am a brother to is Janeane. She honestly is all that i feel is family to me right now. I have some final details and then thats it, i'm done. I'm thru with this family treating me like i'm an outsider, like i'm nothing. My final decision is i do not want the house, and thats final. I am looking on moving from the area. Does that make people happy. The house is all yours Alexis, Chip, Terrie I need none of this anymore. Its a joke, it really is, my dad isn't even gone yet and everyone is worried about Gordie getting the house. I'm gonna be the man of the situation and say i'm done with it. And people stop blaming me for your own faults in life. I'm not god i don't make your choices for you. Just because i have basically lived a straight and narrow, positive lifestyle, does not give people the right to try and mess it up, especially family. Here it goes i'm a man, so if you think less of me about anything come out and say it, don't be a lil punk and hide behind doors. I might not agree with you and your not gonna always be right nor i either, but i will respect the honesty. Seriously i'm tired of

116

*the chickens talking crap and hiding , come out and get
some, i'm right here. My family has a lot of jealous, igno-
rant fakers in it.Is this how we were raised,no, i don't think
so. Now am i a cast away in this family as people were once
cast away for having lepracy? I AM SOMEBODY ,I DID
NOT ASK TO BE A PART OF THIS , I WAS ADOPTED,
NOT MY CHOICE,LIVE BY THE RULES OF ADOPTION.
And one more thing worry about your father instead of what
you think i'm getting. Taking me out of the will seems like
the best thing to do,its not even near that point and its so
stressful. And people wondered why i once put my name as
Gordie X. PEACE BE UNTO YOU BROTHERS AND
SISTERS.*

This cry of pain was anguishing to everyone. Someone said
that adopted children might have an especially hard time with
losing a parent. People tried to reassure Gordie, and to admit
their own grief and anxieties as well.

Meanwhile, Janeane was making plans to come weekends to
relieve Elinor, and Willa was working on the question of
headstones for Sonny's grave as well as Pete's. In the e-mail
correspondence, people asked questions about the medications,
expressed thanks, and were generally supportive.

==

Pete's Progress, February 5

*Hey, y'all, I never wrote up a report yesterday, just too worn
out. And then we had another rough night. It is the*

117

vomiting that is so intransigent. Breathing is getting tougher. Pete's developing sores and thrush in his mouth. And bed sores are threatening.

So today Hospice brought in a hospital bed, with a high-tech alternating- pulse pressure pad, and oxygen. But so far, Pete won't use it. A volunteer masseuse spent an hour with Pete. Both a nurse and a social worker came to consider all the options with us.

All the financial business is completed as of today, and Gordie and Janeane have got plans for the funeral etc. pretty well in hand. So the MD will likely increase the potency of meds now, even if it makes Pete unable to respond much at all. Better that, than this constant pain and retching all day and all night.

Caro (sister) will get here by late tomorrow and is planning to learn the routines so that I can take a night away, maybe Friday. Other visitors are expected, too, later in the week.

All of this is twice as complicated as I make it sound, with errors, malfunctions, misunderstandings, false starts, grey weather, and confusion. In other words, life going on, as Sonny would say.

Terrie and Willa and Gordon and their partners have been in and out, being sweet and helping with things. Alexis and Chip and Celie find mundane little ways to help constantly.

Pete's voice is fading away to a mere whisper. It is hard for him to make himself heard, which is frustrating for all involved. In order to hear him, you have to walk up near to him every time he speaks, and he has to repeat himself.

Pete has had to figure out a good answer for people who ask how he's doing. Generally nowadays, he says, "I'm behaving." Good, huh?!

Pete's got a brusque side and some remarks sting. But most often, he curbs his tongue and is incredibly resilient under this constant attack from the big C. He is not called a "patient" for nothing. So I'm cheering for him.

Cheers.......Elinor

Pete's Progress

Chapter 5: Hospice Residence

Pete's Progress, February 6: Major change

*Dear People, there has been an unexpected change. Pete
has moved to the hospice residence, a six-bed house on a
hill in Concord. It is about a 30 minute drive from his home
in Medford.*

*There were a couple of steps. As you've heard, though
Pete's pain has been more or less controlled, and he hasn't
complained much about more or less starving, the vomiting
and retching have continued both day and night, exhausting
him to the point where he asked Hospice a couple of days
ago to just increase the various meds so that he
wouldn't know what was happening. (He already is very
groggy and sleepy and sometimes a bit delirious with frailty
and meds.)*

*For a day or so, Hospice urged instead that we try yet
another treatment routine, so we did. No good. Again Pete
said, just take this misery away. Hospice staff and I
discussed whether and how I could manage a near-
unconscious patient at home. Someone who cannot get up to
pee or vomit or move around to prevent bed sores.
Then last night, unexpectedly, a bed became free at the
hospice residence. So the nurse came this morning with the*

suggestion that Pete be taken there, so that the sedation he is requesting can be managed appropriately. Pete jumped at it, and kept asking all day where the transport team was. They came at 3:30 this afternoon.

Meanwhile, Alexis and I alerted all the immediate family to the new plans. When the ambulance came, daughter Willa from Concord, and sister Caro from DC were here, ready to accompany Pete to the residential hospice.

Caro is going to stay the night with him, though he has not requested it. Alexis, Terrie and I will go tomorrow morning. Family and weekend visitors will also be able to see him there -- visiting hours are 24/7.

We still have no clear idea of the time line ahead. Hospice workers will continue to offer liquids when Pete "surfaces." (He hasn't kept down any solids to speak of for weeks.) His DNR (do not resuscitate) order is clearly in place. He will continue to be offered all comfort care, including oxygen, but nothing that will prolong his misery. He will not be given IV food or fluids.

Pete knows that all the finances and arrangements are in place. He does not care about such things any more: "You all take care of it," with a dismissive wave of the hand. He is not afraid of dying. He has been clear that there is nothing more he can do for his family.

Pete has requested that portions of the <u>Carmina Burana</u> be played at his funeral. When the house was empty except for me late this afternoon, I played the whole thing, loud, with the doors and windows open, while I straightened things up, *did the laundry and the dishes. The music is a celebration of life, sensual youthful enthusiastic life at that, and this is what Pete wants us to remember in relation to him.*

Cheers for Pete.

Yours....................................Elinor

Pete was not on the waiting list for the hospice residence; he had always said he wanted to die at home. But home was too hard for him. And in fact, he was at home right up until he was so frail and sedated that he didn't clearly know where he was most of the time.

Pete's Progress, February 7

Well, dear watching friends and family, Pete is now established as a resident in wonderfully bright, comfortable surroundings in a spacious house on a snowy hill just south of Concord.

Most of us wept hot tears at the news that he had chosen to go there, because the decision was such a milestone. But it is a pleasant place, appropriate to the increased level of sedation he is under already. The vomiting and retching seem to be stopped!! If Pete is bleary and absent-minded as part of the project, so be it, as long as his distress is reduced.

Last night, Willa accompanied him to the residence and Caro spent the night with him; today Willa will, if it seems warranted. In between, visitors have included me and Alexis, Chip and Lucelia. Tomorrow Terrie will be the first

122

visitor and others will follow. Maybe even Pete's far-away daughter, Jill, will be among them -- she is reported to be on her way here from her father-in-law's funeral in Michigan, on her way back to Louisiana!

We figure a steady stream of family folk coming by for short visits will assure Pete we are remembering him, without wearing him out.

At home, the place feels empty without him. But we remember how he would fret over the thump of the washing machine off-loaded with towels, or the exact setting of the thermostat. The house itself distracted and distressed him -- it was too hard for him to let go here.

There are new noises and protocols for Pete to get used to at the residence, of course -- and also new resources. He was accepting of hospital bed, alternating pressure mattress, and oxygen, though he rejected them at home. At the residence, there is staff awake and on duty 24/7.

The goal of it all is not to prolong his life but just to increase his comfort. How long the road will be still is not clear. So be wishing the best for him. We are all cheering for Pete.

Cheers.................................Elinor

Willa stayed with Pete the second night and sent a full report:

Hello all:

I spent the night with Pop last night. I arrived at the

123

*Hospice Center around 10:30, and found Pop awake and
perched precariously on the side of his bed. He was
agitated, and once he was able to fix on the fact that I was
there, he motioned with his hand that he wanted a drink.
There was a sippy-cup on his tray, so I tried to give him a
drink from that, but he grunted and pushed it away.
Suddenly thinking that maybe (oh dear) it was left there by
mistake by Alexis - who I figured was toting Lucelia along
when she visited - I went out to the nurses station to ask if
the cup was in fact for Pop. The nurse explained that Pop
was often tipping over a regular cup when he tried to take a
sip of water, so they gave him the sippy-cup. I told her that
while I was there I would monitor the water for him, and
she went and got him a regular cup. Sure enough, Pop had
a very difficult time with the cup, but he insisted on holding
it himself. Still agitated, he fussed with the bed table
constantly, organizing and reorganizing his spit bin, his
tissue box, and the cup of water, and moving the table
around here and there as if he needed to get things just
right. Around 11pm the nurse came in and offered Pop the
choice of taking his medication orally or rectally. She
explained to me that he was refusing the medicine rectally,
but he was also having a difficult time trying to swallow the
pills that he needed. Elinor, is there anything we can do
about that? Any liquid medicine possibilities,or perhaps a
medicine port on his wrist to inject meds without having to
stick him constantly?*

*The nurse came back with five pills. Pop wouldn't let her
put them in his mouth; he insisted on doing it himself, but
got angry and confused trying to maneuver the tiny pills on
his own. As soon as he finally got all the pills down he
suddenly stood up and stated very clearly that he wanted to*

go home. I put my arm around him and reminded him that I was there, and everything was okay. At that, he sat back down on the bed again and just looked at me for a few moments. MASH was on the television, and knowing how bothered he is by superfluous noises, I asked him if he wanted the TV off. He shook his head no. After a few minutes he again got agitated and stood up and seemed like he needed to go somewhere. I asked the nurse if she could help him to the commode, and she did, then asked the aide for help in getting him back into bed, which Pop refused to do. He insisted that he wanted to sit in the recliner. Once in the recliner, he got upset about the nurse putting up the footrest, and I explained to her that he didn't like the footrest up. She told me that she was worried about him trying to get up and falling, so I assured her that I would be there all night and I would monitor him. Pop still seemed upset. I decided to switch channels and look for the History Channel, which Pop often watches. Once I found the station and turned down the volume a bit, it was like a magic switch. Pop focused on the program, calmed down almost immediately, and stopped fidgeting. I explained to the nurse that Pop loves that channel, and she was surprised at how well it calmed him down.

I realized that Pop had developed a "way" of coping at home, and when he was situated the same way at hospice he felt "okay" about things again. Just like at home, he likes to sit watching the History Channel with the volume low, with his table at the ready and his water at the ready. When we brought him there, he told me to make sure that they "followed the program, like I do at home." Within twenty minutes, Pop was sleeping peacefully with his hand on his table. I read a book titled "Blink", which Elinor had given to Pop who knows when. A few times during the night Pop would get a mild case of hiccups in his sleep, but they didn't last more that a minute or so. Once in awhile he'd suddenly sit upright in the recliner like he was about to get up - I'd almost jump out of my skin at the sudden noise! Always, however, he'd almost immediately relax again and go back to sleep.

I left around 6:30am and headed back to work, Pop still sleeping and the nurse notified that I was leaving with a reminder that Pop would need to be watched in case he suddenly decided to try to get up.

I thought about death and dying throughout the night, and realized that it seems a lot closer to me now, unlike when I was younger and couldn't seem to imagine the reality of it. Being there with Sonny, and now with Pop, both so alike in how they've weakened and become more and more disoriented, it occurred to me that I was experiencing what it is to "watch over". Just as I watch over my children as they sleep and grow and change and expand, I was watching over Pop as he sleeps and declines and changes and fades. And in both, there is so much love and so much that it is necessary to accept.

Please send your prayers that Pop will go gently, and without fear.

Love to all,

Willa Marie Porter
*Please note that I have added Terrie and my mother to this list; for some reason they were not on it before.

126

Oy! Elinor sympathized later.

"How does that happen? Names just disappear for no known reason. I had constant problems maintaining the e-list. Eventually I think there were 47 people on it. New people kept asking to be added, and their interest and concern was very supportive for us at home."

Here's one from an old family friend. Messages like this were very supportive.

Dear dear Elinor, what an incredible day it must have been for all of you. Sounds like a really good plan. I think your <u>Carmina Burana</u> *story is wonderful, and will remember it (and you and Pete in it) always.*

I'm off to Sare's tomorrow (Thurs), to do whatever is useful, restful, fun, calming, or anything else she can think of! Don't know what each day will bring, but I'd much rather she not be alone a lot until we know better what's happening with the vertigo. Things certainly sound significantly better.

A small note re Pete. You mentioned that his breathing is getting harder. Is the plan to include morphine in his meds? I've had a lot of experience with it in situations like this, used to help breathing rather than primarily for pain. I found out about that from a pulmonologist involved with the care of a close friend who died at our house. To my surprise, her really terrific oncologist didn't think of morphine that way and was not inclined to provide it. It made all the difference in the world for her breathing, calming it down so that her last days were MUCH more peaceful. No doubt you know all that, and/or hospice does, but I mention it just in case someone doesn't know.

As sad as these days are, it's very comforting to think of Pete ensconced at Hospice, as chosen by him, without you having to try to manage a person who can't help himself much. You have been such a trooper--I'm glad the pressure is off you a little. But I've been there and done what you're doing, and I know how exhausting that role is, both physically and emotionally. There's no way this could have been managed without you, I believe, and I hope that knowledge brings you some sense of joy and accomplishment even in the midst of the sturm und drang.

A VERY BIG HUG. And thanks again for keeping me in the loop.

x x x x x x margie

Several people had asked about morphine. When Elinor asked the hospice nurse, he said its equivalent was in the other meds Pete was getting. And Pete never did have serious breathing problems, just tightness in the chest.

======================================

Pete's Progress, February 8

Dear friends and family,

Things are going OK today. Willa spent last night at the hospice residence with Pete, and Caro spent much of the day.

The best good news is that the vomiting and retching have been gotten under control. Pete took pills and drank water without vomiting. Whoopee! This was his major goal in going to the residence.

He is more comfortable there as it becomes more familiar. He is using oxygen very little. He is heavily sedated, as he requested, but is still able to respond a little, to transfer from bed to chair with a "stand-by assist," and to enjoy a little outing to the sitting room in a wheel chair.

The future is unclear, and the hospice staff suggests that care options be reassessed after Pete has been in the residence for a week (next Wednesday) and we at home have had a rest. They seem to suggest a chance that Pete might come home again for a bit, if he can accept the alternating pulse mattress and the oxygen when needed, and if the vomiting can be controlled. The Hospice staff are astounded at how sick he is while still so strong. They don't know what to expect. We'll see. Not knowing and waiting are hard, but we have no choice.

Tomorrow is the big visitation day. Jill is already in town from Louisiana, and will go with Terrie to see Pete. Two nieces are expected here after midnight, and will go with Caro and myself to meet Hunter and Millie, up from Philadelphia, at the residence around noon tomorrow.

We like knowing that all of you are in touch, standing by, sending good wishes, and participating as you are able.

Cheers for you...Elinor

129

A cousin who had never met Pete in adulthood wrote to Sarah:

Dearest Sarah,

The writings from you and your Bowers clan members have brought us great inspiration and hope. If there is joy and hope for us in the future, it seems that Pete is showing the way through his incredible strength and courage. Thank you all for your many e-mails and, would you welcome any visitors to bid a fond farewell to your twin?

Much love, Clark

But at this point, they were turning away all visitors except immediate family. That was hard. Blessings on Clark, he came later, for the funeral.

===

Pete's Progress, February 9

Well, we streamed through Pete's room at the Hospice yesterday as expected. He received us all graciously, though he snoozed through much of our time together, being heavily sedated.

In the late morning, we were Caro, LeNay and myself; Hunter and Millie; Corinne. At about 2:30, this group went for lunch except for Millie, who sat with Pete. We returned to find that Janeane, Jill and Kirk had arrived. Kirk is Jill's big handsome husband of ten years, a long-distance trucker from the west coast who spoke and showed great affection

130

for his mourning wife. Pete joined a family circle in the spacious living room of the Hospice for a bit before we started our departures around six.

The good news was that Pete was not needing oxygen, and took a bit of soup and quite a lot of water during the day. One disappointment was that he experienced an episode of vomiting again late in the day. But the RN on duty this morning says there was no more of that, and that he had a restful night.

The "medicine cocktail" is being lightened and we'll all be watching to see if the nausea cycle recurs or not.

Several family visitors will be in attendance again today, Sunday, and we'll be in touch with the rest of you by e-mail and phone.

Cheers..........................Elinor

Pete's daughter, Jill, lives far away and hadn't been close to the family, so no one had met Doug before. He was very like Pete himself in many ways, and some twenty years older than Jill. It was great to see that she had so strong and fond a husband.

===

Pete's Progress, February 10

Dear friends and family,

131

The real news this weekend is that Gordon set up suppers at 1010 Elm for his siblings and everyone else around, not one night but two. This was the same guy who was so mad at his siblings earlier. Pizza and chicken Saturday; honey-baked ham with macaroni and cheese on Sunday, when Jim made REAL mashed potatoes and provided the beer.

People had come from all over. Gathered around these two spreads, one night or the other or both, were Jill and Doug all the way from Louisiana; Willa and Erin; Terrie (Jim was working); Pinky and Flip from Ithaca; Alexis and baby Celie (Chip was working); Gordie and Prim; Caro from DC, LeNay from Boston, and myself from San Francisco. I could have missed someone. The Saturday party shifted midway to Gordie and Prim's for the NASCAR races on a wide-screen TV, in honor of Pete, who wouldn't have missed them. I think Janeane, Alan, Tommy and Abbie from Scranton joined them there. Kathy, Corinne (New Jersey), Hunter and Millie (Philadelphia) missed these feasts, but had been at the hospice house with us.

Arguments erupted and tears fell, but overall, people pulled together in Pete's name, at Pete's house, and it was a very good thing to be part of. That Beatles' song kept going through my head: "Come together, over me!"

Both weekend days, there were people at Pete's side at the hospice residence in Concord much of the day, and he did well in the care of nurses there at night. No pain, no vomiting, no bed sores, no need for oxygen. Can't carry on a conversation, but he was definitely getting tired of that many days ago.

*All the out-of-towners will be gone by tomorrow morning,
Monday, but Janeane is coming back from Scranton
promptly, to sit with Pete evenings. I can be with
him during the day time. Others will be coming as they are
able. Wednesday Janeane and I will meet with Hospice
staff and assess the situation, deciding whether to continue
as is, or make any changes.*

*On the way to the hospice house today, Caro and I attended
a church in Concord, a very welcome hour or two for me. I
have missed church so much. Perhaps I will be able to go
another Sunday.*

*I appreciate your personal e-mails, but Pete's kids don't get
to see them. Cards would also be welcome. ...*

Cheers...........................Elinor

It turns out that virtually all the support and condolences came
by way of e-mail and phone. The family received very few
cards – times have changed in that way. More cards would
have been good.

===

In Medford, they were still struggling with the idea that Hospice
might send Pete home again. He sometimes seemed to want
that. Sarah wrote:

*I want to suggest that we provide something in writing to
Hospice before their assessment meeting. I admit that part
of it is my own need to feel like I am contributing some of
what I know. I am wanting to help lay out a clear and*

133

specific set of reasons why Hospice provides a level of care that is needed and can no longer be provided at home.

I am sure that we are communicating first and foremost that Pete's returning home is not a good thing for him, that Pete's wish to die makes it very hard for people at home to provide adequate care, that the respite support of Hospice volunteers and family is no longer adequate to support him at home, that there is no question but that every effort must be made to let him stay at Hospice.

I am sure they know that we will provide lots of support for them at Hospice with supportive and committed family and friends.

There is no financial problem with insurance and Medicare fully in place.

The increasing care needs include:
the vomiting,
the falling,
the bed sores,
dehydration,
meds. monitoring,
ambulatory compromise
the limited number of people to help at home,
no one at home who can lift

Elinor wrote back immediately.

Oh, thanks, Sare, this is a helpful strong statement about why Pete should stay at the residential center.

At this point, it is not Hospice but family members who have been wondering if he should return home. He would be easier to care for now than he was before they took him. And he has said to a daughter or two that he wants to go home.

But I still think that the residence is a milestone on the path he is taking, and that it makes no emotional sense to backtrack.

Hospice prefers Pete to be at the residence. He is easier to care for now that he is sedated, and family people are there all the time to monitor and help.

Moreover, Hospice gets an extra $200 per day when Pete is in residence. (I am not sure you are right that insurance and Medicare cover this -- anyway, the family has to pay a good bit. But Janeane, as executor-to-be, has approved the cost.)

But Hospice's position might change if their waiting list presses, so we'll have your list here available...

Many thanks.................Elinor

===

Sarah offered a quiet weekend at her home three hour's drive away, but there was no way Elinor could leave. Even after Pete's death, when she had another chance to visit Sarah, ordinarily very welcome, she could think of nothing except going back home to Arizona.

135

"I realized that I was desperately home sick. Everything about the situation at Pete's was very, very different from my normal environment. In fact, now I might even recommend that a person not take on such an end-life stint unless it could be done from her own home, with her own support network nearby. I got a chance to talk about this a little bit with the hospice social worker, which was helpful."

===

Pete's Progress, February 11

Dear Ones,

It is hard today to think of this passage which Pete is traversing as "progress," as in the title of these reports. Today Pete cannot stand, talk, eat, or readily make his needs known. Fluids in and fluids out is about the sum of it. He responded to two year old Celie early this morning, but after that the day was dim for him.

But he is progressing towards his ultimate destination, as he had hoped. It is our destination, too, which is one reason why we are watching so closely as he models the way for us.

Janeane replaced me at the Hospice residence at about four, which will be the pattern, according to our plan. But we think it will not be for long. There is no longer any thought of Pete coming home again. But there may be changes still in his medical regimen; we'll see.

It is strange to shop and write and do laundry and watch TV, like every other day, when Pete's days have changed so much. But it is our task, I guess, to keep on in the usual way, pretty much. Life goes on, as Sonny liked to say.

I believe the family expectation is that the funeral will be three days after Pete's death. I'll get more information about this tomorrow.

Yours............................Elinor

==

Karen's Aunt Karen wrote yet again:

Dear Elinor,

It appears from your emails that Pete is definitely on the downward slide and that his passing is imminent. It seems that he has gone downhill rapidly since I saw him about 3 weeks ago. Please correct me if I am wrong.

So much has happened to Pete over the years - so many hardships with the deaths of Jeri, Tina and Sonny, and now to have to see oneself be so incapacitated and know that your time here on earth is limited. Your brother is very brave and courageous and I admire him for that. We may not have seen eye to eye on many things, yet he always maintained his easy-going nature and acceptance of things beyond his control in a manner that I tend to be the complete opposite of (and it is hard to admit that I can be quite a hard head). I envy those qualities.

137

Your daily messages at least keep me a part of Pete's final days, and I thank you for including me in this. I worry for you and your family and for Karen, whom I have always considered my "older daughter". I will try to be there for her and you in the end. Life does go on...

Hugs.......... Karen C.

Eliznor wrote back.

Karen, I have really appreciated your supportive messages.

It is great to know that you are talking with Karen Kay. I am not sure who she is in touch with, and I worry that her grief is just a huge lump in her heart as she tries to keep on with her work and her usual life. Do call her.

She is expected here this Friday -- unless Hospice tells us to call for her earlier.

Thanks.........................Elinor

They did call her earlier. They began calling everyone on the afternoon of February 12, to tell them that Pete had died at noon.

===

138

When Elinor arrived at the residence at 11, the nurse was just telephoning her to come—there had been major changes in Pete's condition in the last hour or two. It was true. He looked startlingly different, lying on his back, gaunt and blind-looking, mouth gaping.

Elinor telephoned for his children to come, then went to sit with Pete. She held his wrist (it always hurt him to have his hand held because of the neuropathy), watched his chest rise and fall, and gazed at his changed face. The room was cleared of all meds and equipment except a discreet Foley catheter. It was an attractive, private room, full of light, with snow falling gently outside. It seemed right that his children were not having to sit there for a long time waiting for him to die. Perhaps their presence would have held him back.

It was very peaceful and quiet. Pete's breathing slowed and faded so gradually that it was hard to tell if he was breathing at all, even with her hand on his chest.

The nurse came in and asked if he was breathing. "I'm not sure," Elinor told her, and the nurse brought out her stethoscope. She could still hear a wavering heart beat, but no breath. She left the two quiet together for another five or six minutes, then came back and confirmed that Pete's heart had stopped. Elinor says, "I remember touching her hip as she stood beside me, for moral support, and looking at my watch. It was straight-up noon."

The RN called the doctor in. He confirmed the death and, at Elinor's request, gently massaged Pete's eyelids so that his eyes closed and he looked more peaceful. The doctor could not get Pete's mouth to close. The nurse showed Elinor the mottled markings on Pete's feet and knees which come with death. His hands were slightly curled and cold.

Elinor sat there with Pete for a while, grateful that there were some quiet moments for his body to settle into rest and his spirit to depart, as so many cultures believe important. It was a sacred moment, and she was not afraid or sad. It seemed almost more than chance when, within days, she came across this passage in a book of Jane Smiley's.

> *Honey, the best thing to do with a dead body is to sit with it for a while. Til you get used to it. If someone else is around, you should both sit with it, and chat about what that person was like. In my experience, if you can just give yourself time to get used to the way that person is now that he's dead, or she's dead, then all the rest comes easier. Dead bodies are quiet. That's comforting, in a way.*

Sarah, his twin, got a quiet sort of pleasure over the fact that Pete had been born on 12/2 and had died on 2/12. The years were 1945 and 2008.

==

Pete's Progress, February 12:

Well, most of you know by now, dear friends and family, that Pete stopped breathing at noon today. It was my privilege to be with him, holding his hand and watching his face and chest. So I can assure you that he just faded away, breathing less and less often until he breathed no more. No pain, no agitation, no anxiety or gasping for breath.

We were able to just wait in silence for a little while. I had already called his local children and knew they were on their way to the Hospice residence. Various hospice workers came by to pay their respects, and then the family started to gather.

We family people had two hours there together, taking turns in the room with Pete, and sitting together in the lounge area, sharing tears and hugs, making phone calls.

Slowly we started talking about what would happen next. Janeane and Gordon had already laid out general plans with the funeral home, so the details were now worked out.

There will be "calling hours" from 6-8 on Thursday. The funeral will be on Friday at 1:30, with Sarah leading and opportunity for people to share memories. Those two events will be at Samuelson Funeral Home at 11 Manning Street in Medford.

If you can come, please also come to share potluck afterwards at Pete's house. The burial of Pete's ashes will be in the Medford Rural Cemetery later in the spring.

Karen and Roger are expected to get here from DC later this evening. Curt and Sarah will come Wednesday or Thursday. Holly's whole family is planning to be here from Massac husetts by Friday. We are waiting to hear from others. We have room at Pete's house for a few who bring sleeping bags -- let us know your plans in advance by phone or e-mail.

141

In various places in Pete's house, there are badge-type pins which read in part, "Enuf is enuf." I am wearing one tonight in Pete's honor. He has done enuf.

Love....................................Elinor

They never said what he died of, at the end. No vital organ – heart or lungs or kidneys – actually failed. Perhaps he died of starvation. Perhaps the death certificate reads "complications of cancer."

Pete's Progress

Chapter 6: Funeral weekend

There was a paid obituary in Concord paper.

Pete S. Bowers, 62, of Medford, NH, died Tuesday, February 12, 2008 at Hospicare in Concord after a extended battle with cancer.

Born Dec. 2, 1945 in California, he was the son of the late Eberling and Margaret Bowers.

Moving to Medford in 1978, he worked as an auto mechanic, and later for BART. He was an active labor organizer, making numerous trips to Washington, DC to rally for issues of concern to nation-wide unions.

Pete is survived by his children (theyb were all listed) 18 grandchildren and 1 great grandchild. His brother, Hunter Bowers of Philadelphia, his twin Sarah Bowers of Winbrook, NH, his sisters Elinor Bowers of San Francisco, CA, Holly Bowers of Boston, MA and Caro Green of New York City, and several nieces and nephews survive him as well.

A celebration of his life will be held on Friday, Feb. 15th at 1:30 p.m. at the Samuelson Funeral Home, 11 Manning St., Medford. Family will welcome friends on Thursday evening, 6-8:00 p.m. at the funeral home.

Burial will be held at a later date in the Medford Rural Cemetery.

The funeral home took responsibility for the obituary, preparing a draft at the last minute from information provided by the family. This corrected version of the obituary appeared in one of the local papers, but another version full of errors got printed in the other paper.

The family found it hard to get the basic material together. Children often do not know much about where their parents have worked over the years, and only Pete's siblings knew the details of his birth date and place. Pete had outlined how he wanted the funeral to go, but not how the obituary should read.

Pete's children also had trouble figuring out how to contact important people about the death and funeral. There was a rolodex, but no way to tell which were Pete's friends. E-mail was even more challenging. First they had to find the password to Pete's e-mail list, and then, again, it was impossible to tell which names referred to people who should be notified. The children started working on this two weeks before Pete died, but it was already too late for him to provide any guidance.

There were questions about how to inform Pete's former wives and partners. His daughters figured it out somehow, and also got the news to his old tenants, in-laws, relatives of several sorts, one or two neighbors, and all the people on the long family list.

===

Pete died on a Tuesday. The plan was for the commemorations to include "calling hours" with the body on Thursday and the funeral on Friday. There was a sudden whirl of arrangements for the extended family people who would come. There were many e-mail exchanges and phone calls. For example, from Holly:

What I'd like to know is: What is the name of the hotel/B&B in Medford where Pete and Jeri spent their wedding night? Does it still exist? I'd thought to stay there if we could? If it is no longer open, I wonder if there is a place (or two) in Medford (1st choice) or Concord (2nd choice) where other family members are staying where Ken and I might find a room as well.

Also, is there any floor on which my girls might sleep? Shanta will only be there over Friday night. Eliza may be there over Thursday and Friday nights. (She's not sure yet about Thursday.) Lauren will be there for the funeral but will not stay overnight there ever.

Thanks.   Love,   Holly

Elinor responded, and then Holly wrote again:

Thanks for this. You will have read my other email by now, too, about the Bell Gardens Inn. We will bring air mattresses and sleeping bags for Shanta and Eliza just in case.

We will be arriving with Rob and Cissie (family friends) in time for the visiting hours. Eliza will not arrive until 10 pm or so. Shanta and Lauren will arrive late morning on Friday.

I am burned out. Sarah is burned out. You are near

*collapse. But we will all recover and our lives will resume
and offer some solace by next month or so. (Maybe sooner!
Hope springs eternal, right?!)*

*Ha-ha! I already told Ken that we had to bring wine and
specifically sherry because I, like you, discovered when I
was there in December that there is no potable sherry to be
found within a 30 mile radius of Medford! Forewarned is
forearmed. We'll come prepared.*

I am so immensely grateful to you, Elinor.

Love,
Holly

Several people wrote that they could not attend but would be
thinking of every one and of Pete.

==

Pete's Progress, February 15. (There were no reports on
the 13th and 14th.)

*Dear people, half of you on this list have been here last
night and today, and many of you faraway ones have sent
flowers, photos and greetings which were welcome.*

*Thursday night there were "calling hours" at the funeral
home, where Pete lay in state, looking wonderfully restored
to a condition he had not known for many months. On the
pocket of his short-sleeved blue shirt, he wore his pin
reading "Enuf is enuf." His big, black, brimmed hat was
laid across the casket above his knees. The <u>Carmina</u>*

146

Burana played in the background as we talked, cried, admired photos and shared reminiscences.

The group of us occupied all the beds and sofas in the house and many in local guest houses and motels. We included all Pete's siblings, their partners, most of their east coast children and their partners. All Pete's children, their partners, and most of their children were here. Karen's in-laws live here in Medford, and were with us. Samantha and other friends, neighbors and past tenants of Pete came. Our long-time family friends, Rob and Cissie Enman were here. Our first generation cousin Clark came to represent his side of the family. Peter Stimpler was deeply involved in everything. Friends of Gordie Bowers attended. They will all have different reports about this same event.

The funeral home directors had known Pete for 27 years, and participated as friends as well as official hosts. Karen Kay and Sarah, Pete's youngest daughter and his twin, led us in a memorial service where all were invited to speak their memories of special times with him. Many people did so, with tears and laughter, and we got a full-fledged and colorful overview of Pete's life that we were happy to celebrate.

The celebration spilled over to Pete's house afterwards, and the contributed food kept us busy for a long time.

As I write, many people have dispersed to homes near and far, one group has gone to the Moosewood Restaurant in Concord, and a half dozen are chatting in the living room here. We found a letter Pete wrote recently to his great-grand-daughter, Lucelia, age 2, which I will copy for you

*tomorrow. Then I'll go home Sunday, and this chapter will
come to an end.*

*As executor, Janeane will take the lead as Pete's children
sort out his belongings and divide his estate--the next
chapter in the same story. May it go well for them.*

Cheers......................Elinor

Does it sound calm and sweet? But of course, extended family
life being as it always is, there were many layers, many
complexities.

- Many in the family are not accustomed to open
  casket ceremonies and were more dismayed than
  reassured by the sight of Pete's fresh and youthful-
  looking body displayed in a glossy casket
  surrounded by flowers.

- Pete's explicit instruction that he be laid out in a
  working man's shirt with his wide-brimmed rustler's
  hat on the casket at his knees caused comment both
  favorable and bemused in this family which
  struggles with its own class divisions.

- The fact that Pete's body was so transformed since
  his children saw him gaunt and grey and gaping on
  his death bed three days earlier caused two reactions.
  One, the morticians did a fine job at their task. But
  two, there was a huge disconnect between what the
  local family had experienced at the hospice and what
  the out-of-town visitors were seeing in the casket.

- The family neglected to plan for the Friday morning after the calling hours and before the funeral, so a good opportunity for family visitation was lost.

- Very few townspeople or local friends and colleagues of Pete's attended the calling hours or the funeral, whereas his children had expected a throng. There was much conjecture about the short-fall. Was Friday afternoon a bad time? Was there not enough advance notice? There should have been a better address list to work from. Had Pete's colleagues forgotten him in the year since he had stopped working? Or had he annoyed people? And why did it matter anyway?

- Pete's twin, Sarah, facilitated the funeral gathering in a democratic style, allowing anyone present to stand and share memories of Pete. She appeared to become faint at one point. Her son stood behind her with his hand out to prevent a fall; her daughter knelt next to her and held her ankle – a poignant scene, another reason for tears. Was it not right to ask her to fulfill this leadership role when it was her own twin they were memorializing?

- But the messages people offered were varied and fine, rich with tears and laughter and even some plain-speaking about how hard life with Pete had sometimes been for his children.

- One of his several past partners was there, speaking her truth to the family for perhaps the first time ever. (Perhaps it was hard for some to hear.) She and Pete had lost a two-year old, and her testimony described a healing gesture he had recently offered her.

- The funeral home was spacious enough for the large gathered family. But the house, where pot-luck food was shared after the calling hours and, next day, the funeral, was very crowded, overwhelming some people.

- The usual family divisions were evident in the way people coalesced into sub-groups. Local family members, the ones most bereaved, slipped away from the gathering pretty early on.

- But generally, people were well satisfied with the "send-off" they had provided for Pete.

Daughter Willa gave a lovely, straight-forward message during the funeral in place of a reading from the Tao Te Ching she had meant to bring with her. A couple of days later, she e-mailed the reading to the big family-friends list and thus initiated the memorials-by-e-mail which preoccupied everyone for a few days.

Celebrate Paradox!

No-thing remains itself.
Each prepares the path to its opposite.

To be ready for wholeness, first be fragmented.
To be ready for rightness, first be wronged.
To be ready for fullness, first be empty.

To be ready for renewal, first be worn out.
To be ready for success, first fail.
To be ready for doubt, first be certain.

Because the wise observe the world
Through the Great Integrity,
They know they are not knowledgeable.
Because they do not perceive
Only through their perceptions,
They do not judge this right and that wrong.
Because they do not delight in boasting,
They are appreciated.
Because they do not announce their superiority,
They are acclaimed.
Because they never compete,
No one can compete with them.

Verily, fragmentation prepares the path to wholeness,
the mother of all origins and realizations.

Verse 22, Tao Te Ching

Translated by Ralph Alan Dale

Someone found Pete's letter to Lucelia, written a year earlier
and published in a book called *Love, Grandma*. [There were
about 25 grandmothers and one grandfather, Pete himself,
featured in that book!]

Dear Lucelia, my great-grand-daughter,

I, like you will, grew up in a family in which money was not
seen as the most important value in life. In fact, my parents
(your great-great grandparents) followed the Quaker way of

151

simplicity. They eschewed taking more than needed for a comfortable and peaceful life. I thought I should have more things when I was a kid, but as I grew up, I realized that being able to appreciate the true value of things led to an easier life.

Somewhere in my teenage years, I read about Native Americans and what impressed me, and stuck, was their attitude about possessions: rather than "owning" things, they lived with things. The indigenous people of this part of the world valued things and plants and animals as a part of the whole of creation with an equal entitlement to the joys and benefits of life,

Ever since then, I have just lived with things, not really owned them. In fact, sometimes I think that the things I live with, like my house, own me, because so much of the time and money I have go into the taxes and maintenance of the property.

This idea of respect for other lives is a part of real Christian religion ...at least if you read the Bible from the inside out. Most people begin with the book of Genesis and the stories about God's division of the firmament into light and darkness and heaven and earth, and His making of animals and people and everything. ... But [I like to read the Bible starting] in the middle, in the middle of the New Testament, in the middle of the book ascribed to Matthew, in the middle of the 5th Chapter, at the 13th verse, where it says, "Ye are the salt of the earth; but if the salt hath lost savour, wherewith shall it be salted?"

Reading on from here, I learned a radically different way to experience life. The words are ascribed to the man called Jesus, often called the Son of God. But it is the words, the ideas, the principles, the attitudes, the intentions of these writings that I find important. Everything else I read in the Bible, I read with these things in mind.

Here, in the "Sermon on the Mount," is the root and the foundation of everything in your life and experience that has the family name of Bowers attached to it. As you encounter a difficult and confusing world, I hope you will hark back to the middle of theBible and refresh the very essence of your being as the salt of the earth. There you will find affirmation of who you are and reassurance that even though you are different from your peers, you come from a long tradition of righteousness.

At first these things, these radical ideas of righteousness, seem impossible and difficult and unrealistic and daunting. But as you put them into practice in your everyday life, they empower you and sustain you and invigorate you and protect you from all manner of adversity and unpleasantness. While you may not reform the world, you will improve the little bit of it on which you can have influence. And while the world may seem to crumble around you, you will know that you have tried and you will be at peace.

May the strength be with you, for goodness sake.

With much love and best wishes for you and your world,

Your great Grand Papah

Medford, New Hampshire, 2007

Despite this letter, Pete claimed he was not religious, and he refused any kind of minister or Biblical references for his funeral. But the extended family includes many faiths and practices, so it was good to hear from niece Lauren.

Pete: Blessed be the God and Father of our Lord Jesus Christ, which according to his abundant mercy hath begotten us again unto a lively hope by the resurrection of Jesus Christ from the dead, to an inheritance incorruptible, and undefiled, and that fadeth not away, reserved in heaven for you, who are kept by the power of God through faith unto salvation ready to be revealed in the last time.

I love love love you all so much. God bless, xoxo -Lauren

==

Each family member will have his or her own story about the funeral gathering. The scene that stayed with Elinor was her sister, standing so pale and faint, with her children in their new role as her care-givers.

"It made me fear again for her well-being. It made me consider how my own children will be required and inspired to shepherd me along this same path Pete has taken."

Hard stuff. Where in this new "line" do the rest of these six siblings stand? Pete was the fourth child. Elinor remembered him on the phone six months earlier saying to her, "Hey, you were supposed to be first, you're the eldest."

"Yikes, so sorry, but who can tell? I am guilty about being so healthy, four years older than he!"

These events made another sister think a lot about becoming an end-of-life support for her husband. His hopes and expectations about life after death are not quite like hers. Will that make any difference?

Pete's Progress

Chapter 7: Grief and reassurance

The visitors had gone and Elinor was leaving New Hampshire, but the story was not over. Suddenly there was much grief, confusion, sorting out to be done. And the estate, including Pete's house, had yet to be settled.

What with the February weather, it took Elinor thirty hours to get back to Arizona. Ideas and feelings swirled in her head like the snow storm outside. In an airport along the way, to clear her mind, she wrote down some of the things she wanted to learn and remember for her own last days.

- Settle all your affairs, write your will, and tell all your children clearly about everything before you get too frail to do so.
- Clean up your place and toss out the junk if you can.
- Draft your own obituary and outline your own memorial service.
- Specify where you would like commemorative gifts to be sent.
- Annotate your address book and e-mail list so that family can tell who to contact when you die. Make sure the family can access your e-mail address lists.

- Give little mementos from among your things to friends and family members during the last year of your life.
- Don't insist on dying at home – it is too hard to let go of your responsibilities and your life in such dear, familiar surroundings.
- Don't have someone from far away be with you for more than a week or so – it is too hard for them to be "a stranger in a strange land," without their usual support network.
- Use hospice services, but help the family have appropriate expectations.
- Realize that control of pain and nausea has to develop by trial and error.
- Expect grief, confusion, guilt, and resentment to plague everyone during the last days, and to explode right after the death.
- Expect other family issues and events to get all mixed into the process.

Regarding little mementos, Elinor did take three for herself, with Janeane's permission. She took the little plastic measuring spoon she had used for weeks as a med cup for Pete. She took an old-fashioned wooden darning egg which had originated with the grandparents and ended up in Pete's house, though no one there knew what it was for. And she took Pete's bathrobe, the one he had worn all through their weeks together.

==

Gordie wrote to the whole family again, again in a swivet of grief and anger. It seemed as though he and Terrie were the only ones among them all who could really express their turbulent feelings. Or was it that, being adopted children, they were feeling this loss more than the rest? Gordie had the

157

impression that the family home was going to go to granddaughter Alexis, and was fiercely resentful. Many people wrote to reassure him.

His sister:

Gordie, do you think that Alexis is not grieving? Yes, Alexis is my daughter and you are my brother. But listen up, it should not be about who's grieving and who's not grieving. And who's getting the house and who is not. I don't know what to say, I read your e-mail and it makes me sad to see that you can be so mean. Come on Brother, we all loved our <u>*Pop*</u>*.*

A fond uncle:

Gordie,

Chill OUT! Is it possible you're jumping the gun?.....Normally there is a will and an executor (sometimes two) appointed by the deceased while living. The executors actuate the will and carry out legal necessities of which there are many. I assume any such will written by "Pops" is fair and equitable to a fault.

Everyone needs to cooperate with these intricacies and poisoning the waters real or imagined at this stage will only serve to complicate the logistical realities.

Check the baggage at the door and pull together as a family.

May your rewards be great.

Uncle Stu

And then a cousin, another guy Gordie's age and race, in California, sent a long letter. Here's an excerpt.

> *So just hang in there guys and don't worry about getting screwed over or the short end of the stick because it doesn't matter that much. Gordie if you're feeling betrayed by these people, give your self some space from them and do your own thing, don't worry about what they are saying or doing, do your thing and take care of Gordie and Gordie's wife and let things cool off and settle down, emotions are wayyy raw right now, but you know you are all basically good people and no one truly hates anyone.*
>
> *Ok much love to all of you guys, I obviously was not there for the funeral physically but my heart and thoughts were there as much as anyone else's, I loved Pete as much as anyone and miss him and am happy that he is resting in peace, after having lived a huge life and done so much for so many people, lets try and carry on his tradition of love and giving and peace, lets not tear down and burn any bridges just yet, we'll all be fine in a little bit of time.*
>
> *Stay Up and Much Love,*
>
> *Boy-o*

Gordie's aunt Holly wrote to Gordie with copies to all, reminding him of the death of the family patriarch, her father and Gordie's grandfather, always known as DB.

Dear Gordie,

Being his sister, I obviously do not have the same feelings about Pete as you have. But I can tell you that, although your father was not my father, I also had a father who died. I was 40 years old at the time. Day after day I tried to carry on normally with the business of life, and day after day I found that I was completely preoccupied with the memories of my father. It's important and necessary, I believe, to grieve and to process the deaths of people who are important to us. (And who is more important than a parent whom we credit with having shaped us?)

I read books about death. (On Death and Dying by Elisabeth Kubler-Ross is a particularly good one.) ... [Then I decided] to write down everything that had been going round and round in my head. I ended up writing a 30-page typewritten thing about the last 21 months of my father's life ...

After that, I found that thinking of my father was like opening a huge, heavy, iron door. It was a struggle to open it. I left it shut for a long time. When I finally mustered up courage and strength enough to open it just a crack and I peeked inside, at first it was too painful to look, and I quickly let the door clang shut again. As time wore on, though, I could open the door more easily and when I looked inside, what I saw was his loving eyes, or his hearty laugh, or...you know...all your fondest memories, instead of the painful things.

[There is a] temptation ... to collapse under the weight of your grief. But this is a pain that we all go through ... and

*God won't allow you to suffer more pain than you are able
to endure. He will provide a way for you to bear it. Pretty
nice, eh?*

The diversity of temperament and reaction, not to mention age
and race, seemed quite marvelous to Elinor amd made her very
fond of all this extensive family.

She wrote to them all.

Dear Friends and family,

*Hey, it is more than a week since I left New Hampshire and
still I am spending hours, day and night, thinking about the
convoluted rich experience we have been through together.
I'd wager many of you are doing the same, especially those
in Medford.*

*Pictures flash through my mind – Pete on his knees by the
toilet, Pete getting loaded into the ambulance, Celie coming
to say "night-night," Alexis and me in our pajamas drying
up water from the kitchen floor after the dishwasher
flooded, Pete waking me at 4 am (what, again?!) this time
to admire the full moon shining on the new-fallen snow. On
and on. Are you having flash-backs like these?*

*I think and think about all the ways in which family
members helped get Pete what he needed, about how
hospital and hospice served us well despite their mistakes,
about all the complex aspects of family relations that were*

expressed during the calling hours and funeral. Are you thinking about all this, too?

I ponder about where fear and anxiety emerged among us, about our communication problems, about previous deaths we have known, about all the new things I learned about Pete's life. Some of you share these thoughts, I know.

I wonder about the future, how you who are Pete's children will divide his assets and make use of the new opportunities that result, how we who are in Pete's generation will deal with our own illnesses, how all of us will walk the road to death when our time comes. All of us share these preoccupations just now. ...

Sarah and Elinor talked and talked by phone about Pete's life, what had been the dynamics from childhood, what had seemed to go wrong, what worked well, how in the end, as he had said himself, "It doesn't matter." They figured other family members were also doing this inevitable review, not to judge but to seek all the possible lessons from a life just ended.

Granddaughter Alexis wrote a sweet sad letter to everyone which she titled "Day by day":
:

As I sit here trying to somehow put everything together, I get reminded by this house that my grandpa is not coming home. I remember him saying to me for the last three weeks, "It's not going to be long now." He was talking about dying. I told him that he had told me this before, and he said, "Yeah, I know, I just want you to get used to the fact that I am not going to be here anymore."

I think no matter how many times he said that to me and I replied I am going to be alright, I just can't get it in my head that he isn't going to be calling my name to ask me some question or ask me what I wanted to do for lunch or what my day is going to be like, or what are you burning (that was a famous question of his whenever I was cooking something).

I think it is just the constant reminder of being in this house that is making me so sad or my little two year old asking me everyday where her Pop Pop is and telling me that he will come home after I explain exactly what my grandpa wanted me to tell her. I told her last night that her Pop Pop would come home if he could but he can't, after she was looking for him again to give him a kiss goodnight as she always did. She just looked at me in this sad face and I told her it is okay to be sad because mommy is sad too and so is everyone else that loved Grandpa.

She said to me, being the smart girl that she is, Well why can't he come home, where is he? I told her the only thing I knew, someplace where he feels better and where people go when they die. I told her that I am not sure what that place is called, but that I am sure it is a good place and that I am sure that Pop Pop is okay. I told her that Pop Pop was old and was sick for a long time but reassured her that Mommy, Daddy and her still have a very long life, and we will get better when we are sick. After that long talk, I could tell that she was still confused, but then she just gave me the biggest hug and told me it is going to be okay. So it is the next morning and she hasn't asked me yet. (Thanks, Aunt Sarah, for the advice.)

It is funny how my day goes now, I do a lot of pacing because I feel I am not as busy as I used to me. There is something missing but maybe once I have this baby that missing piece will be there. I sure it will be. Grandpa often told me when he found out that I was pregnant, that this was all going to work out because I am going to need that baby once he is gone, and that he was so happy that I was going to give a new life while his was slowly going away.

As some of you might know, I haven't changed the answering machine yet. It feels good to hear Grandpa's voice still on the answering machine. I know I need to change it but it makes me feel safe in a way and I am afraid if I change it I will forget his voice.

Well, that is how I am doing and it is nice to read all of your emails. I will keep you updated on the baby news.

Lots of love
Alexis

Then Elinor found in her e-mail files another gift for everyone from Pete. She shared it with everyone.

Look at this, guys -- just found in my e-file for Pete, written by him to nephew Harry (and copied to many of us) on October 1, 2006:

Harry, I cannot speak for everyone, but for myself, I can say that when one is faced with imminent death one generally remains the same person they have been. People often die with the same hang-ups, prejudices, biases, misconceptions,

164

illusions, revelations, expectations, and so on that they have at the time. Life has been what it has been and at the time of death, there is no more time to make it different. Acceptance is easier than rejection and remorse. I hope that I will be remembered in favorable ways: good person, man, father, husband, lover, employee or employer, landlord, great grand father, son, thinker, politician and much more. I hope my errors and deficiencies will be forgotten (pointed out, but forgotten). In fact, I have that hope at all times.

I hoped that my children would turn out all right and they have, but each is what they are, not what I made them. My influence has been variable and unpredictable. I have given what I could. Society, education, experience, brain structure and capabilities form all of us and we are all part of each.

I can hardly hope to have made the World a better place. It is only in my own small corner that I have aspired to affect the environment around me. ...

All the best to all, and best of luck, for luck is a bigger part than all the rest. Look down from the Sun and you will know this. Look up from the beginning of time on Earth and you will know this.

Luv,

Pete

Gordie reminded Elinor and Sarah of C.S. Lewis, author of the most famous book in the literature of loss, called *A Grief Observed*. When his wife died, back in the sixties, using a pen name at first, Lewis poured out his anguish and pain in this book. He couldn't sleep, he could hardly stand. His children were of no comfort and his friends were an irritant. Though a devoutly religious man, he lost his faith in God. Then slowly, slowly he gained his balance again.

Gordie was in the worst depths of grief when he wrote these words:

> *Yes, i too have been thinking of our father and i figured each day would get a little easier, but instead its harder I keep thinking he's going to ride his motorcycle into my apartment complex just to stop by and say hello. Anyways like today my wife went to see her father, so i was home alone i got mad then i got sad, and mad again, and then i just cried. I miss him so much. ...*

> *Anyhow what i'm saying is i'm hurting, and i'm hurting a lot. But i know that i remember everything that my dad had ever said to me his family, all the fun, all the negatives, everything, and i will never forget him. He is what made me be what i am today, tomorrow and the next, let me rephrse that, he will guide me still. I will miss his talks, his lectures. Oh God, this is so hard, I really do not fear anything, but what i do fear is when this all finally sinks in, and i fully believe that he is gone and never coming back.*

Again there was a flurry of comforting messages. Everyone was so glad when Gordie's mood shifted. He wrote about the Georgetown basketball game, where he was the hero and the

166

father figure for young boys. The Pete within him came to the fore.

It was Saturday, the 16th of February, we had just put our father, grandfather, brother to rest the day before. I was heading to the Georgetown-Syracuse game. I for one did not think i was going to be able to go, I have not missed a game there in like 16 years. The last 6 years or so my father had accompanied me, this was dearly missed. I had thought about purchasing tickets for like 2 months, i would go on and then i would say no. I had a weird feeling our father was gonna pass around this time. I finally thought about it and said, he would want me to go, so i bought the tickets.

Now the price we won't talk about, cause the normal person wouldn't buy them. I bought two first, 4 rows from the court, to the left of the Georgetown Hoyas bench, boy was it hard just trying to find someone that could go and wanted to. I was very picky about this, because in a way it was Pop's seat.

Anyhow i then got an idea i coach summer basketball to kids that don't get all the fanfare as do the richer kids in the school. I said why don't i take a couple from my team that i coach. So i got online, and purchased 2 more tickets. I called the kids, and talked to the parents, they were fine with it. The two kids couldn't wait. Of course i had to supply some Gtown t-shirts too.

Now its Friday night still no one to go with Pops ticket. I know what your all thinking, why not take your wife. Well, i would have, but she knows i'm a nutcase, especially if they lose. Anyhow, its now morning time of the game, I ponder a

*bit. There is lil Tommy, Janeane's son, my lil cute nephew.
I had asked him before but he didn't sound to sure, so i
asked him again, he said yes. See the whole thing came
down to, i wanted someone to really appreciate the game
and remember it.*

*So we traveled to Syracuse, Oh i forgot Tommy needed a
shirt, it was very cold, so i gave him my blue
Gtown sweatshirt, it fit him like a lil blanket. Well we got to
the stadium with no traffic problems. Tommy couldn't
believe how big it was. Once we got inside, the first thing we
did was get something to eat.T hen we went to look at our
seats. Now my kids from the team are really pumped, they
have heard from me that i talk to the kids on the team and
have talked to the coach, but they didn't really believe it.
Well they did when we first walked down the stairs towards
the court and who is standing there talking to the press. The
Hoya coach JT III, he sees me and immediately waves
asks how i've been and of course i say good and you. Then
he had to go back to the locker room. My kids were like oh
my god (in my terms oh my gosh). So i said wait till the
players come out. Well they did as i shook hands and
slapped fives, and called them by their names, and the few i
talk to, said wuts up. This whole time my kids were ecstatic.*

*Then out of the blue, this lady comes up to me and asks me
questions, basically interviewing me for <u>The Georgetown
Press</u>. She asks how long i have been a fan and who i knew,
and who was the superstar. I was like wow, i'm being
interviewed, if my dad could have been there, he would have
had that great smile he has when he is happy. So then that
was done, so we watch the players warm up a bit, figuring it
was done. Then she comes up to me again, and says can this*

168

guy interview you, i say sure. So he asks me why i like the Hoyas, and i say what i say to my own team, they think about education first, and athletics last. And that anyone who goes on that team and stays 4 years graduates 95% of the time. They also take young men and turn them into quality people. Then they take a couple pictures of me. I was shocked didn't know what paper it was going in, but didn't care either. After that we went and sat down.

Well the game starts, and its Gtown leading and then Syracuse just couldn't miss. By halftime we're losing by like 21 points. It was cute watching Tommy, i had to lift him up to be on the chair. There was one time i'm not sure what channel, but Tommy and i got on T.V. The guy looked at us said 3-2-1 and pointed to signal the camera was on. Tommy had never been to a place so loud as he plugged his ears for most of the game. There was like 32,000 people.

Anyhow Gtown didn't give up at all, they cut that 21 point lead down to 5, but it was too big of a lead to overcome, so we lost. You know what, for once, i wasn't even angry. As we left the game all the fans were taunting us, i just said enjoy the nit, which is considered the losers bracket of the NCAA , cause gtown will be heading to the big dance known as March madness, coming soon to a city near you. And hopefully a trip to the national championship.

Well, i asked Tommy if he had a lot of fun, he said ya, so thats all that matters. The kids from the team, heck, ya, they had a blast. Now i'm debating on a trip to D.C., for the louisville-gtown game, possibly a title game for first place. Anyhow thats all people, hope you enjoyed my lil story. Bye for now.

The family loved that letter!

===

Caro sorted out the question of commemorative gifts, and sent out a message to the whole list.

In consultation with others, it has been suggested that contributions be made either to Green Peace to acknowledge Pete's deep and long-standing concern for the environment, or to your local hospice out of gratitude for the hospice care that Pete received in his final days.

Thank you for your kind thoughts.

Janeane, Pete's daughter and executor, reassured Elinor with the following note. Really, all that mattered now was that she and Pete's other children were feeling OK about how things had gone.

Dear Aunt Elinor,

Thanks so much for taking these weeks out of your life to help your brother and our family. As I sit here sorting through estate, I am feeling that things are in pretty good shape. The bills are paid, the accounts are in order. Our father passed away with the love and support of a multitude of family and friends around him. These last few threads are precious and I am lucky to be able to be involved and will handle with the gentle care that Pete would have.

170

I am going to sit down with a financial advisor and explain the needs and the opportunities. I am fairly confident that the abundance of loaves and fishes that was left to us will be sufficient.

I don't think Pop will ever really leave us. He is part of all that we are and we can't change ever.

Alexis wrote about sending the coat Elinor had left in her car at the airport, and added a bit.

I have gone back to work. Chip stays home with Lucelia during the day until someone calls him back on a job. He has never had this much trouble finding a job and he is disappointed but it will work out I think. He said he really likes to stay home with Lucelia and didn't realize how much stuff I actually do every day. He says he has a closer relationship with her already, I think he always had. It is great to be back to work though ...

Mom [Terrie] is buying the house! She is renting the other half to me for a while. I hope it works.

So at least the family didn't have to give up the house yet.

==

Sarah wrote to Elinor and sparked the idea of recording this story in some form.

What a hiatus away from home.....before it fades, I hope you get it down....You have the facts -- catch the feeling of it.

Well, most of it was already written down, because it was all in the e-mail file.   Maybe with a little help, it could be captured and woven together to share with others…..

About the author

Elizabeth Boardman has published several other books, always helping to make known the ideas and writings of others.

Her first book originated in her trip to Baghdad with a peace team in December 2002, just before the Iraq war. It is called *Taking a Stand: A Guide to Peaceteams and Accompaniment Projects*.

Another book, *Where Should I Stand? A Field Guide for Monthly Meeting Clerks,* is of special interest in the religious community of Quakers to which she belongs.

 I'm Not a Tourist, I Live Here! is a delightful collection of stories about life in San Francisco.

Made in the USA
Charleston, SC
04 January 2017